I love this book because it is s[...]
honesty and pain choked me, o[...]
at myself, at my nation with ou[...]
sense of humour. From toilets t[...]
to religious observance, sarcasm [...] self-deprecation, queuing to cricket,
not to mention language, class and vicarage oddities – it's all there – all the
British foibles that make other nations think us bizarre. To see yourself as
others see you – ouch! And yet, in Amy's gentle hands it's a revelation –
funny, challenging, surprising, chastening and cheering.

Read and enjoy. You will. As I turned the last page, I could only say,
with profound thankfulness, that America's loss has been our gain.

*Michele Guinness, author and speaker*

Reading Amy's book left me feeling tender. Not only because we live parallel lives, but also because it's a poignant illustration that whenever you
follow God's call after the dream, there is the *reality*. There's always a difference between the two; it can leave you disorientated, uncertain of who
you are and what you're doing.

It's here that Amy's beautifully written book offers such rich treasures.
Her journey and reflections remind us that whatever the call – a new relationship, a new job, a new community or even a new country – our
adventures with God bring both unexpected sacrifices and sorrows and
unanticipated blessings and breakthroughs. Most of all, Amy helps us see
that through all life's seasons we are held and kept by the love of a faithful
God, that in him we lose and find ourselves, and in him we are home.

*Jo Saxton, speaker and author*

What a joy it is to peer over Amy's shoulder and enter into the seasons of
life through her eyes. I found myself drawn much deeper into the question
of what makes us who we are wherever we are. Amy is not just a social
commentator, she is a discoverer of life and meaning, and her reflections
invite us all to create memories and a place called home – wherever we are.

*Cathy Madavan, Digging for Diamonds*

*Finding Myself in Britain* offers a delightful and insightful view of life from
both sides of the Pond. The author's honesty, wit, and warm personal reflections draw the reader into her world, and her love of history and the

church broaden and deepen her observations. I was especially taken by her through-the-year approach, highlighting each season – an ideal way to capture the beating heart of each country. In a word, I loved it.

*Liz Curtis Higgs, best-selling author,* Thorn in My Heart

Candid, funny, poignant, engaging, and always brilliantly written – *Finding Myself in Britain* is a marvellous read. As Amy tells her story she opens up a way of seeing the world in which we are all strangers somewhere, yet we can all feel at home. This Englishman-in-America loved it.

*Os Guinness,* The Call

You don't have to be an American to enjoy this book. Or British. Or a vicar's wife. You just have to be somebody who has found themselves in an unusual place, felt a bit out of their depth, and wondered where God was in all of that. That's most of us, I think.

*Bob Hartman, storyteller and author*

Amy has given us the gift of a beautiful book. Warmth without sentimentality, engaging in a "I can't wait for the next page" way, rich in truth, this hopeful, honest book is a treasure trove. Stop pondering the possibility of purchase. Buy it right now.

*Jeff Lucas, author, speaker, broadcaster*

My fellow Anglophile Amy Boucher Pye has written a delightful book that shows how Americans fall in love with their Mother Country. This book is compelling reading for those who want to learn how Brits and Americans can understand – and even like – each other more.

*RT Kendall, minister and author*

No matter what your background or where you come from, you will find yourself in Amy Boucher Pye's book. It is a wise, funny, and thoughtful examination of how life circumstances bring unexpected blessings.

*Katharine Swartz,* The Vicar's Wife

(Endorsements from the first edition of *Finding Myself in Britain*.)

# *Still* FINDING MYSELF IN BRITAIN

## MY SEARCH FOR FAITH, HOME *and* TRUE IDENTITY

### AMY BOUCHER PYE

Authentic

First edition published 2015 by Authentic Media Limited,
52 Presley Way, Crownhill, Milton Keynes, MK8 0ES.
authenticmedia.co.uk

Second edition published 2025 by Authentic Media Limited

**British Library Cataloguing in Publication Data**
A catalogue record for this book is available from the British Library.
ISBN 978-1-78893-445-9
978-1-78893-446-6 (e-book)

Some names have been changed,
and some stories are composites of several narratives, but all come from real life.

Cover design by Vivian Hansen

To Nicholas, without whom these reflections wouldn't exist,
and to PyelotBoy and CutiePyeGirl,
our amazing Ameri-Brits,
with faith, hope, and love.

And to my family in the States who waved me goodbye,
not knowing if or when I'd return.
Our days are in his hands.

# CONTENTS

*Foreword by Paul Kerensa*                                      ix

Introduction: A Stranger in a Foreign Land                       1


**Part 1:** Fall into Autumn                                    13

  1   "More Tea, Vicar?"                15

  2   The Day They Buried Diana         23

  3   School Days                        34

  4   "We Will Remember"                 44

  5   Bringing in the Sheaves            50


**Part 2:** Winter Wonderland                                   63

  6   Life as a VW                       65

  7   Waiting for the Coming King        75

  8   The Light of Christ Has Come into Our World   84

  9   The New Year Dawns                 96

 10   Come to My Party!                       104


**Part 3:** Marching into Spring                               111

 11   By Their Accent Shall Ye Know Them      113

 12   "Behold Your King!"                     122

 13   Being Easter People                     132

 14   Festival Time                           142

 15   Plumbing the Depths                     148

**Part 4:** Summer Nights 155

16 Rain, Rain, Go Away . . . 157

17 The Rhythm of Rest 166

18 What's in a Name? 173

19 Queuing, and Other British Sports 180

20 Parallel Lives 190

Epilogue: Liquid Love 209

Afterword 218

Recipes 229

Acknowledgements 266

Notes 268

Join the Conversation! 280

# FOREWORD

Lose yourself in a good book, they say. And if you're going to lose yourself, I can't think of a better book to find yourself in than this one.

Amy Boucher Pye's fish-out-of-water tale is superbly relatable yet uniquely insightful. We won't *all* move across an ocean to marry a Church of England vicar (though if you are, wow is this the book for you . . .) – but we can all empathize with that odd feeling of being a stranger in a foreign land. Make that a hope-filled American experiencing bizarre British life, and you have before you a few hundred pages of joy. Amy has both a way with words and a great perspective on her own journey. She knows her heart, and is willing to share it with her readers. That's you, and me. We're a lucky bunch.

I haven't found myself in another culture or continent to the extent that Amy has. I grew up in a tiny Cornish village, where "travelling" meant visiting a bigger Cornish village.

The longest I've spent in another country was a road trip across the United States, from coast to coast to coast. We managed 37 states in just over a month, and (for some unremembered reason) filled a bottle of Atlantic water to later release into the Pacific. I've felt guilty ever since at whatever untold ecological effects we caused (probably zero).

Along the way we toured, we drove, we attempted to find some real America. I don't know that we fully succeeded. While in search of the average, we felt drawn to the super-latives. The world's largest pitchfork? Welcome to Casey, Illinois (who also claim to have the world's largest rocking chair, knitting needles, Dutch wooden shoes and more). The world's smallest horse? Texas State Fair claimed to have it. I paid my five dollars to see . . . a Shetland pony. I guess in a land of stallions and mustangs, such a small beast – common in Britain – was worthy of fame across the pond. I suppose Sir Walter Raleigh's first potato in England once got looks. I don't know if he thought to charge a fiver to look at it.

Off the beaten track in rural Pennsylvania, we met some regular Americans who recognized us as outsiders – due to our rental car's Connecticut number plate. When we our opened our mouths, they were amazed at our accents. "Do you know Prince Charles?" was the first question (that dates it). "Have you met The Beatles?" was next.

The Pennsylvanians asked where I lived, and I soon found myself explaining what a semi-detached house was. "You share a wall?!" came the incredulous reply. "Marge! Quick, over here! This British guy shares a wall with his neighbour!" (Although I sense he didn't spell it like that.)

He proceeded to tell me how we should move to Pennsylvania, how they could walk around their house on either side, and how this was really the key difference between UK and US housing. "I can turn out my front door, turn left OR right, and still end up in my back yard!" I recall him saying.

So back here in the land of back gardens rather than back yards, Amy has chosen to make her home. And my brief trip Stateside gives me a very basic understanding of the cultural differences Amy's faced over the years, going the other way around, for a lot longer – for a whole new life. Although as a Christian, Amy knows that any new life here on this earth is nothing compared with the new life that awaits us if we trust in Christ.

Amy is well-travelled and well-read, though she wears it lightly. In this book she effortlessly channels Dante, Brother Lawrence and Samuel Johnson, but doesn't make us feel bad for having not read them.

She wears her faith on her heart and her heart on her sleeve, so wherever you are on your faith journey, immerse yourself in Amy's. It may help prod at what you believe about Jesus, who he was and/or is, and who we are as a result.

Oh, and there are recipes (or do Americans call them receipts? We can't even agree on what that's called). Something for everyone – whichever side of the Atlantic you find yourself on.

So welcome to a book that I know will become one of your favourites/favorites – and indeed U are in it. (So yes, British English spellings are throughout, so it's "colour" not "color." We'll let Colorado stay as is – though on my road trip I did add the odd "u" to some flyers to make it Colourado, trouble-maker that I am . . .)

Enjoy this book – I know you will. Lose yourself in it. Find yourself in it. Have a nice day, and God save the [insert monarch here].

*Paul Kerensa*

# INTRODUCTION:
# A STRANGER IN A
# FOREIGN LAND

We bowed our heads in prayer, the convention centre dimmed, tens of thousands of university students gathered. When the leader asked for people to dedicate themselves to world missions, standing to signify their commitment, I heard Lynette next to me rustle and move. As she made her public declaration, I felt no urge to join her. In contrast, I felt called to stay; called to pray for renewal and revival in America. In conversation with friends I would trot out an oft-employed line, saying, "I want to support God's work here. So many people are committed to serving other nations – and that's great. But I don't want to forget about our home country."

Then the leader asked for all who felt called to support those going out in missions to stand and show their commitment. I rose to my feet, wanting to uphold Lynette in her work. She was dating an MK (missionary kid) who had grown up in the Philippines, and their plan was to marry after she graduated and make their life in that tropical island.

We'd gathered to learn about world missions, with the theme based on the Old Testament book of Jonah, entitled "Should I Not Be Concerned?" I didn't realize at the time that

I was a lot like Jonah, who went to the people of Nineveh after much wrangling, even jumping off the side of the boat to avoid his calling. For yes, I wanted to be concerned about the world, but no, I didn't want to uproot my life and go.

But eleven years later, that's what happened.

I met him at a book club, on a Saturday night. I was annoyed over the book we had agreed to read, and why have book club on a Saturday night, anyway? Trying to quash my attitude, I greeted Chris, a friend who attended the local Anglican seminary.

Chris said, "Amy, meet Nicholas Pye. He's here this semester from England."

A man beamed at me from across the room. "Hello," I said. "So you're at seminary with Chris?"

"Yes, I'm an ordinand in the Church of England."

"You're studying for the ministry?"

"Yes, I'm an *ordinand* in the Church of England."

Not sure what he was meaning, and seeking to move the conversation along, I said, "How are you finding life in DC?"

"Wonderful. But I didn't realize I would need a car over here so much. I've been stuck on campus for six weeks with only other ordinands for company."

More friends arrived, and I turned my attention elsewhere before we got down to the business of discussing *Sophie's World*. As usual, we split along gender lines, this time with the men liking it and the women not finding it as engaging. Finally I couldn't contain my annoyance any longer. "Okay, so I've been peeved at this book counting as one of our *fiction* titles. I only read fifty pages before giving up – it's just philosophy masquerading as a novel!"

Two of the guys exchanged glances. "It *is* a novel," one of them said. "Just a somewhat demanding novel."

I huffed and complained but after a while realized I should quiet down and let the conversation continue. They discussed Sartre and the Renaissance, the Enlightenment and medieval times. I kept thinking, *"I'm so not into a discussion about the history of ideas. Not on a Saturday night!"*

Later, as I took off my makeup and got ready for bed, I replayed the evening and heard how whiney I sounded. I realized I should have done better with reining in my tongue, and planned my apology to the hosts the next day. I grabbed the novel I was reading, *The Divine Secrets of the Ya-Ya Sisterhood*, relieved not to be pondering philosophy any more. But that evening changed my life.

Reader, I married him. In a historic (for America) Anglican church we joined our lives in sweet matrimony. The courtship and engagement whirled past, including several visits to the land in which I would settle, but I had no idea what life was really like on the other side of the Pond. My prince had come, but I struggled to understand the kingdom.

As I think back to those early days, I see myself timid and mute, afraid to speak lest my Americanness be revealed. Growing up, I had always been the good student, the one not to rebel. But here, by my very nature I was different. I'd see people translating my words when I'd say "tennis shoes" or "diapers," and I quickly tired of asking them to repeat themselves when I couldn't grasp their accent or understand their words. Looking to the television or newspapers for comfort didn't satisfy either, for the few TV channels boasted shows with humour I didn't get, and the newspapers' columnists were unfamiliar.

Life was a mixture of sweet and hard. With Nicholas finishing off his theological training in Cambridge, I lived my first seven months in Britain in that rarefied place of evening prayer under the fan vaulting of King's College, tourists punting on the River Cam, a daily market, and the nearby thatched cottages. I knew that transitioning to a new culture would be tough – my English-boss-in-America had counselled as much – but I didn't realize it would be so challenging, or that I would feel like I was losing my identity. But in losing ourselves, we can find our true selves.

My years in England have revealed to me the truth that we're all strangers in a foreign land, longing for our true home. We're pilgrims on this journey of life, and often we face roadblocks and yearnings and pain and separation. But we also experience joy and hope, and we can do so even in the midst of the challenges we face, whether missing our loved ones, battling through a tricky divorce, praying for a child wracked with self-harming behaviours, or coping with disease.

I found myself in Britain. And yes, I mean that in both senses of the word – like the beginning of Dante Alighieri's *Divine Comedy*, "I found myself within a forest dark . . ." And also in finding who I am; landing on my identity in Christ.

In my twenties, a painful broken engagement had spurred me to search out who I was before God; who I was in God. Realizing that I had nearly joined myself in a covenant commitment to a man who was a wrong fit for me drove me to examine prayerfully the deeper issues lurking in my soul.[1] In doing so, I came back to God's foundational truths about how he has created us, loves us, and redeems us through the death of his Son on the cross.

Each morning I would wake and pore over the Scriptures, the words sparking to life as I felt God's gentle whispers of love and affirmation. Like the Psalmist, I found these words sweeter than honey;[2] they were like food to my soul. Waking up early in the morning didn't seem a sacrifice to eat this rich fare.

Those years in my twenties, the Lord was putting into me a new heart and a new spirit; he was sprinkling water to make me clean not only on the outside but on the in. Each day he showed me how he had made me in his image; how he loves me unceasingly; how he'll never leave nor forsake me.

But the story didn't end there. That essential work set me up for my life in Britain, though of course I didn't know it at the time. For when I first moved here, my confidence took an almighty knock as I reeked of self-consciousness as a transplanted American. I felt my ways were being questioned by those around me, or that I was fitting their image of a Yank. Who was I? I knew I was made and loved by God, but how I lived out that identity in this new country I wasn't so sure.

I took years to overcome that painful walking alongside myself, as I observed my words, accent, and actions from the point of view of my new countrypeople. At first I didn't realize I was living this split existence, but slowly I saw the error of my ways and sought God's help to turn from this habitual practice. Living in the present – indeed, "practising God's presence" in Brother Lawrence's memorable phrase – helps me to remember who I am and who lives in me. It helps me shed a dual approach to life.

We don't have to be a foreigner in a strange land to live without living; to pick apart our experiences and conversations; to feel unaccepted or not at home. We all long for love, and we all yearn for community and being known and understood. And this is what I have found in these isles.

Finding myself in Britain has surprised me, for this experience shows me how God's foundational love sets me up to love his people and his world: how he helps me look outside of myself to others as I seek to share his love. How to serve, making a cup of tea for my son when I'd rather stare at my device or fetching a set of church keys when I'd value a few more minutes in bed. How to love as I am loved.

When Nicholas and I contemplated marriage, we each went on a quiet retreat to pray and seek God's guidance about the potential union. I finished my time away on the Fourth of July, later joining the throngs celebrating Independence Day with fireworks, food, and friends on the Mall in Washington, DC. But that morning I was in rural Maryland, reading about Abraham, the stranger who lived in a foreign country. The text of Hebrews 11 came alive in an amazing yet disconcerting way, for I felt that I, too, was being called to a new land.

As Nicholas was studying to be a Church of England vicar,[3] I knew that in melding our lives together, I would need to be the one to leave behind my life in the States. But until that retreat, I hadn't considered the deeper implications of what such a move might entail. I hadn't noticed before that Abraham was *obedient* in going to this new place: "By faith Abraham, when called to go to a place he would later receive as his inheritance, obeyed and went, even though he did not know where he was going" (Hebrews 11:8). In the flush of the first stages of romantic love, it didn't seem a hardship to be obedient to a move to a foreign land – especially such an exciting and olde worlde place dripping with history as Britain. I was blissfully unaware of the costs involved, and that my obedience would need to come later in accepting, with grace and without bitterness or complaining, what I had signed up to.

Like Abraham, I didn't know where we were going; Cambridge was the first stop, but that would be for only a short time while Nicholas finished up his studies before ordination. I didn't know then that I would be moving four times in five years, and thus would be a wanderer like Abraham. This moving brought upheavals and uprootedness, but over time God answered my pleas for belonging, a few friends, and even a fabulous job.

But on that Independence Day what struck me deeply was that I was leaving my earthly citizenship behind – instead I'd be a foreigner and stranger and would need to claim my heavenly citizenship. Like the heroes of faith listed in Hebrews 11, I would be looking for a country of my own; a "better one – a heavenly one." I would have my American passport, and eventually a British one too, but my heavenly passport would denote my defining identity. As, of course, it is for all Christians.

And so this theme of strangers and foreigners reverberates in my look at life in Britain. We can all feel a stranger at times, whether we encounter an uncomfortable work situation, feel like an outcast at church, are the newcomer at an exercise class, stand at the school gate while eyeing the group of close-knit parents, or feel alone and forgotten in our homes. But life is about community, and so I invite you to journey with me – strangers who I hope will become friends – along the A roads and country lanes of this green and verdant land, the rolling countryside dotted with sheep and shining with rapeseed. Maybe we can stop off for a cream tea at a National Trust house, or for a bag of chips by the seaside, or for something warming to sip by the fire in a cosy pub with flagstone floors and low beams in the ceiling.[4]

I hope that as you read, you'll sense my love and admiration for both of my countries, the land of my birth and the land of my adoption. Being an outsider has helped me understand who I am and some of the reasons why I act and think like I do, and has also shown me some of the quirks, foibles, gifts, and strengths of the countrypeople who now hold a special place in my heart.

I've used the seasons of the year as a guide for exploring life here in the UK, from Harvest to Remembrance to the Queen's Speech to Mothering Sunday to Wimbledon. Dotted throughout the seasonal chapters are some topics that Anglicans might say fall in "Ordinary Time": plumbing, accents, and the weather, to name a few.

I hope that you'll grab a cuppa and explore with me some of what makes this country special – a great land of strength, faith, decorum, and wonder. I've found deep and lasting relationships here; a profound love for and commitment to God; a fascinating history that stretches back for centuries; ways and means of doing things properly; heart-enlarging culture that includes music, drama, film, literature; and so on, and so on.

As you read, I hope and pray that you'll feel the loving call of Home. The home we make on earth that hearkens to the Home we long for in heaven. And supremely, the Master Homemaker, who formed us and loves us, and in whom we find meaning, joy, rest, and peace. With him we are at home – in whatever country we reside.

Ten years have swished by since I first wrote this introduction, and Reader, I am still finding myself in Britain. As I reflect on *Finding Myself in Britain* ten years on, I invite you to consider a few themes that run through the book, which you might also find yourself in, starting with identity.

When I first moved to the UK from my home in America, I often felt self-conscious. When I noticed raised eyebrows or pursed lips I'd wonder if I was making some kind of cultural gaffe. Not wanting to offend, and yearning to fit in, I would rein in my exuberance and chattiness or my chortling laugh. After the encounter I'd pick apart my actions and words, wondering where they'd landed and why. Without really realizing it, I shrank into myself. I made myself smaller, not wanting to stand out.

Have you felt this way? It doesn't take moving country to wonder if we're getting it wrong, to want to avoid calling attention to ourselves. But over the years I've come to understand that we're best when we're truly ourselves, not "editing" who we are, walking alongside ourselves, but living freely. I've journeyed to this sense of freedom through finding myself in God. It's a mind-bending notion, but when we lose ourselves, we find ourselves because of Who we find ourselves in – the One who made us and loves us unendingly.

Jesus spoke along these lines as he sent his friends out to share the good news, saying that any who lost their lives for him would find them (Matthew 16:25). I haven't lost my life in a literal sense, but I can see how living in England has helped me to shed some of the dead skin that clung to me as my true self has emerged. I've found myself in Britain as I've figured out, with God, who I am in this culture as a foreigner-turned-friend. We learn who we are in community, and I trust that I'll keep on finding myself as I share and pray and talk with others.

I trust that you too are finding yourself, wherever you make your home, whatever your stage of life.

Along with identity, another theme interlaced in these chapters is home. As I moved, all those years ago, from the home I made in the suburbs of Washington, DC, to England, I longed for community, security, and safety. I wanted to be able to exhale in a space where I would be loved, affirmed, and cherished. In this I know I'm not alone. Whether we live in the same village or town in which we were born, or we've moved from city to city, we all yearn for home.

For me, finding home has entailed sinking into the embrace of God, the ultimate Homemaker whose love cushions the harsh experiences we encounter, the disappointments we endure. When we long to be fully seen and understood, we can trust the promises of the One who made us and who celebrates our unique characteristics.

Although we know and trust in God, we can still struggle, making our homes imperfectly. Perhaps, for instance, we lash out at those we love and with whom we share space, perhaps motivated by fear or insecurity. But when we root ourselves in belonging to God, finding our home in him, we can more easily ask those loved ones to forgive us. To notice when we are acting out because of unmet needs. To lean on God's love and protection as we seek to live in love and grace. We find our home in the God who made us and knows us. In this we can join with the Psalmist in saying:

> You've made me and created me – even all my insides. You've knit me together when I was taking shape inside my mother. I praise you because I'm fearfully and wonderfully made! (after Psalm 139:13–14).

In September 2016 the headlines announced the coming of the iPhone 7, a mass stabbing at a shopping mall in Minnesota, a bombing in Davao City in the Philippines, and *Game of Thrones* winning an Emmy. Meanwhile, in Swanwick, Derbyshire, at the Christian Resources Together gathering, I sat in the the the darkened hall, packed with hundreds of booksellers, publishers, and fellow authors, my heart pounding.

The presenter said, "And the winner is . . ."

I caught my breath as I waited for her next words, wondering if those sitting next to me could hear my heartbeat. Opening the envelope, she said, *"Finding Myself in Britain!"*

Time seemed to slow as I turned to my publishers and hugged them, with Donna grabbing my hand as we sailed up to the front to receive the award for the best Christian living book of 2016. As I gazed out at the sea of smiling faces, so many familiar, I felt a rush of joy. This gathering of publishing and retailing professionals was one I had attended yearly, first as an editor before moving into being an author. In those early days I never would have dreamed that one day I'd stand there at the front, elated at this accolade. That my book connected with Anglophiles and Brits delighted and humbled me all the same.

Coupled with this special recognition, I've been grateful for reviews and letters by readers. I've loved hearing how the book has resonated, not only with people in Britain and America, but in many in other countries. I didn't imagine I'd be writing to younger people, and so a letter from a thirteen-year-old moved me: "My family and I moved from Canada to Scotland last year and that move was incredibly difficult for me. With everything from trousers to toilets to quiet churches, I've felt so lost. Reading your book helped me to look at why I've felt that way and to think through the different aspects of living here and now in Britain. Thank you so much!"

And a note that made me feel so seen came from an American friend who had never visited the shores of Britain. She brought to life the wonderful connections writers and readers can have when they spend time together. She said, when reading, "I was virtually sitting in your home and being hosted by you. You poured your heart into it and I felt that embrace. Everyone who reads your book can experience your hospitality."

I hope that's what you experience as I welcome you to dip into life in the UK from this American's point of view. At the book's end, my modern-day self will meet you at the epilogue, where I explore the themes of faith, home, and identity over the past decade. Think, for instance, of some of the pivotal events over that span of time, such as Brexit, the pandemic, and the cost-of-living crisis, or everyday pleasures such as weekly episodes of *Call the Midwife* and *Downton Abbey*.

Superfans might notice that I've kept the original monikers, Joshua and Jessica, for our children's names in the book. When I first wrote I felt protective of their young selves, not wanting to reveal their identity when social media seemed to be so influential. Now as our kids launch into adult life, I want to bless them in their own ventures, allowing their lives to be their own.

I hope as you consider various quirks and customs in Britain – from plumbing to accents to tea and queuing – you'll sense God's gentle and loving invitation to find yourself in him.

# PART 1
# FALL INTO AUTUMN

# PART 1
# FALL INTO AUTUMN

# 1

# "MORE TEA, VICAR?"

Shall we begin with tea? After all, it's a starting point for much of life in Britain.

When Americans think of English tea, they often picture a posh afternoon event at a fancy London establishment: a three-tiered tray laden with beautiful cakes, scones, and strips of crustless sandwiches; a silver teapot from which loose tea leaves are filtered through a special strainer by a waiter clad in livery; and fine bone china teacups to lift daintily with a raised little finger. This image leaves scant room in their minds for such things as builder's tea, green-crockery-church-hall tea, or first-cuppa-of-the-day tea.

Indeed, that was me, a single woman living in the suburbs of Washington, DC, who didn't consume or understand tea. But one day, that all changed when I opened my door to an English guy bearing flowers. His hair was greasy and he sported a misshapen sweater vest,[1] but I reminded myself that he was from a different culture so who was I to judge? We were supposed to be enjoying this first date at a mutual friend's house, but they were ill and I was struck down with a virus too.

So I invited Nicholas to lunch, serving a fine pea-and-ham soup that he later told me he only just managed to eat. After our soup he asked for coffee, but I had none. Knowing that he was English, I offered him tea.

I made him a cup of my best Good Earth tea – think caffeine-free and wonderful spices. He poured some milk in it and, not surprisingly, scowled at the taste. So I scrounged up the sticky container of loose-leaf Jacksons of Piccadilly that I had purchased on my trip to London, wondering how many years ago that had been. (Please don't judge me – not quite ten.) Rummaging around in the drawer for the teaball thingy and stuffing it full of the tea leaves, I filled the small decorative teapot I had been given for my birthday, which I'd never before used, with hot(ish) water and shoved in the teaball. With a flourish, I presented my guest with the tea tray.

While the tea brewed, I decided to pounce on the opening he'd left in the conversation. I asked a probing question about his family life and he paused, weighing his options as he began to pour the tea. The beautiful teapot, handcrafted, appeared not to be something for use in daily life. Very strong, somewhat tepid tea splashed everywhere, giving him a few minutes to think before responding to my question.

He answered, sharing of himself, and the conversation deepened, signalling the beginning to the end of my single life.

Subject: Tea
Sent: [after two months of dating] To: Nicholas Pye

Darling

I'm sorry to trouble you but I remembered what I wanted to ask you. I went to the store tonight and was going to get some tea. I thought I should get loose tea, yes? Is that better? And what kind? English Breakfast? Or Earl Gray? Tea bags aren't appropriate, are they? Or would they do?

love Amy

"Polly put the kettle on; Polly put the kettle on; Polly put the kettle on; we'll all have tea." I discovered that the British even have a nursery rhyme about tea, for they put the kettle on when they get home or at set points of the day: first thing in the morning and at four o'clock in the afternoon, most universally. After all, drinking tea is a national institution. I've heard of the surges of electricity across the country when all the kettles are turned on after the King's Speech on Christmas Day, or at the start of half-time during the World Cup. I haven't reached the fifteen-to-twenty-cups-a-day level of some of my adopted countrypeople, but I do enjoy a cup or two on most days.

The British obsession with tea remains, even if some of the younger, cool set aren't addicted. When I asked friends what they liked best about tea, a few quipped, "When it's over and I can get back to coffee!" But that's the exception, for tea is served to friends, family, and acquaintances, whether they are popping over for a chat or catching up after church.

And let's not forget the workers who install new floors and radiators; I didn't always know the connection between tea and builders. When we moved into the vicarage, Nicholas was off at a leadership conference, leaving me to deal with the guys laying the carpet and doing the repairs. I was eight-and-a-half months pregnant and not feeling well when I overheard one of them say to a new arrival, "You can't get a cup of tea around here for anything." Mind you, no one had asked me for a cuppa, but realizing I'd made a cultural gaffe, I hoisted myself off the sofa and rectified matters. Since then, I strive to make good tea for those providing services in our home, not least as a means of practising hospitality.

As I ponder the national obsession with tea, I search for why it's rooted in the British consciousness. One reason must be the weather. When you're living in a climate where the damp gets into your bones, and you struggle to get warm no matter how many hot-water bottles you attach to your body or how many layers you pile on yourself, a hot cuppa spreads its warmth from within. I wonder, too, if the British chose a favourite drink that would differentiate them from the coffee-loving Continent. Of course, the rebel colony now called the United States loves coffee for similar reasons – we dumped over that tea in Boston in our own kind of tea party and have never looked back.

Linked with history is culture. Various upper-class women are named as the creators of the practice of afternoon tea; the one I've heard most often is Queen Victoria, who would feel peckish between the long hours between luncheon and the evening meal and would call for a cup of tea around four o'clock. But more people credit one of her friends, Anna Maria, the seventh Duchess of Bedford, as the originator. She yearned for something to pick her up in the afternoon, and turned to a cup of Darjeeling and some small bites of cake. A lovely custom was born.

I'm not surprised that the upper classes came up with this practice, for tea used to be wildly expensive. I've been through country houses where they proudly display the ornate locked wooden boxes where the tea was stored, to which only the lady of the house held the key. The servants, in contrast, had to settle for a weak cup made from the used leaves.

But did you know that the tea bag was actually invented by a New Yorker? How ironic is that – a Yank came up with a major time-saving invention for his cousins across the Pond. And like many innovations, it came about by mistake. Thomas Sullivan was a tea importer, and one day in the early 1900s he sent out samples of tea in silk bags. Although he intended for his recipients to open the bag and remove the tea leaves, they threw the whole thing into the pot. The tea bag was born, depriving rose bushes everywhere of compost material.

Tea bags rose in popularity in the States in the 1920s, but the British viewed them with suspicion, not wanting to mess with tried and true methods of making tea. Only in the 1950s, after shortages from the war eased and new conveniences were introduced in the home, did the tea bag increase in popularity on these shores. Now it's eclipsed loose leaves and is ubiquitous with our tea-drinking experience. We can't overlook the ritual involved when making tea.

Habits are hardened over years of practice, and when we're offered a cup of tea not brewed to our wishes, we might find it difficult to swallow. Early in our marriage, I tried to make Nicholas's first cup of the morning. I brought it up to him with a spoon in it, but quickly found out that the spoon leeches precious heat, making the cup substandard. But over the years I've developed equally strident views, for Nicholas stirs a tea bag far too much for my liking, making it too bitter, which then requires too much milk to balance out all those tannins.

Making tea in a pot entails its own ritual. Warm the pot, boil the water, stir the tea. Serve and then add the milk, or pour the milk first? I've heard that previously people used to add the milk first, because the fine china was more prone to crack when boiling liquid was added to it, so the milk already in the teacup would prevent a breakage. But others will argue vehemently for tea first, milk afterwards, even looking to science to back them up (calling on shades of denatured proteins and other technical terms).

Whether tea bags or leaves, sipped from a mug or fine china, tea signifies comfort and refreshment for many. A friend tells me she enjoys the chance to put up her feet on a recliner, shut her eyes for ten minutes, and rest before the delightful but taxing onslaught of her visiting grandchildren. The first cup, first thing (which has to be in her favourite mug) for my sister-in-law gets her going and keeps her going throughout the day. For a friend in Coventry, a cup of tea, a good book, and a biscuit help her relax. An author friend says there's something deeply comforting about a cup of tea; the calm and the moment to stop, breathe, and pause life. It's reassuringly gentle when life feels too much, making her go "ahhh."[2]

I'm told that more troubles have been aired and sorted out over a hot cuppa than we'll ever know. For instance, some couples take a tea break during their arguments, enjoying a time of relaxing and strengthening before getting back to the serious business at hand. I wonder if they stew while sipping, planning their next verbal lob, or if the tea break diffuses the heat of the fight.

And I've learned that in Britain, hot, sugary tea is prescribed for shock, a practice that may have evolved during the Second World War. As a friend who grew up in wartime London said, the kettle was "always on the hob" and "the tea strong, sweetened with condensed milk. There was no fresh milk and food was scarce. So hot, sweet tea kept us going, children and all! Steadied the nerves (bombs, injuries, deaths) and provided instant nourishment."[3]

I didn't understand the strengthening nature of tea when giving birth to Joshua, our firstborn. The midwives decreed, during the middle of labour, that we should take a tea break. I'd been in the country for six years but I didn't partake, thinking it was a bit ludicrous to stop labour for tea. So while they sipped, I suffered in silence, perhaps a wee bit martyrish. But I should have joined them, for after giving birth I fainted from loss of blood and not eating for too many hours.

Because many people in Britain associate tea with comfort, offering tea to someone becomes an act of hospitality – especially in this climate. A friend likened a British cup of tea as the equivalent to offering a cup of cold water in biblical lands – in the respective cultures, both are a means to relax and revive.[4] Those entering Christian ministry are instructed not to underestimate the value of sharing tea with someone going through a difficult time. Indeed, Roy Godwin in *The Grace Outpouring*[5] recounts how offering comforting cups of tea is a key part of their ministry on the hillside in Wales where God has sparked spiritual revival, not least because of the welcoming nature of the drink.

In terms of offering hospitality, inviting someone round for a cuppa entails less commitment than an invitation to a meal – it avoids negotiating tricky issues such as, "Is this a family dinner? Should I dress up? Should I bring a bottle – but what if they don't drink? What if we run out of things to talk about?" And, for introverts, "How long will I need to stay?"

Thus sharing a cup of tea can provide a building block for friendship – through it we can open our homes to strangers, engage in non-threatening chitchat while arranging the biscuits and waiting for the kettle to boil, and then sit down to get to know our new friend. Enjoying a cup of tea together can thereby provide a safe place to open up and share from the heart. Many times when a friend and I talk over our steaming mugs, the conversation deepens and we move to a time of prayer. Yet only in writing this chapter did I realize how much God can use the humble national drink as an invitation to connect with another.

I was clueless about tea back when I made that truly horrible pot for my suitor. Now I am fully initiated, having witnessed the wisdom of actually boiling the water, for instance, when making a cuppa. I apologize on behalf of my countrypeople who serve you a cup of tepid water with a tea bag sitting on the side; I know now that will just not do.

But how in all this have I not mentioned biscuits?[6] Do you indulge in one with your tea? Biscuits are not something I crave, having not grown up with them. To me, chewy cookies are nearly the pinnacle of baking products, with the winner being cake with buttercream frosting.

Learning to enjoy a cuppa has been part of my adapting to a different culture. I appreciate tea as a means of communion and sharing, a way to reach out to others in friendship – and a means of receiving the gift of hospitality. It's not much of a stretch to say that in its humble and everyday manner, this nation's favourite drink has taught me that my way of seeing and doing things isn't automatically the right or accepted way.

I think it's time to put the kettle on as I consider how to recount the story of what happened the day they buried Diana. Will you join me, especially if I promise not to use tea that's a decade old?

# 2

# THE DAY THEY BURIED DIANA

Like many Americans, I was fascinated by Diana, Princess of Wales, when I was growing up. Not that I would have called her by her proper title when living Stateside – she would have been Lady Diana, or Princess Di, in common Yankee parlance.

When I was 14, we watched the majestic scenes from St Paul's Cathedral and thought it was a fairytale wedding, complete with shy, virginal bride and if not a dashing prince, at least one who had an actual claim to the throne – something we Americans had eschewed several hundred years before, but the pomp and circumstance of which we loved.

I wasn't as Anglophile as some, but I would read snippets about the British royalty in the newspaper or hear about their lives on the news, the glamorous Diana catching my attention as she radiated beauty and contentment even when pregnant. Through the years, however, we started to get a whiff that things weren't all "happy ever after" in the palace. The fairytale evaporated into infidelity, an eating disorder, the infamous

*Panorama* interview, divorce, the stripping of her title, her new beaus, and Charles returning to the love of his life.

Diana was a figure of interest, but one who had little impact on me. I saw her glamorous image and wondered about her privileged but tragic life. I never actually heard her speak until many years after her death, when I caught a glimpse of a rerun of the *Panorama* interview. When she died in the car chase in Paris, I was shocked and saddened, listening to the news reports for hours with Nicholas. But it was the day of her funeral when her persona jolted me out of any mere curiosity or sorrow from a distance. She changed from a distant public figure to one who swayed the heart of my would-be fiancé when he gave her the dozen roses I had thought were intended for me. Join me in northern Virginia, 6 September 1997.

"Hey!" I said when my best friend Kristen picked up the phone. "Soooo . . . he's going to propose tonight!"

"Really! How do you know?"

"Oh, I can just tell. He told me to get dolled up tonight. I'm going to paint my nails – want to show off my ring!"

"I'm so happy for you, Amy. It all goes so fast. Try to enjoy this special time."

"Thanks, sweetie. I'm glad you've done this before me."

As I hung up, I mulled over the day's events. It had started early, at 4 am, when at Dean and Lyle's house we all watched the funeral of Princess Diana. Lyle had served homemade scones, jam, and cream, and Nicholas hadn't mentioned that the English tend to eat those only during afternoon tea. She had made such an effort to reach out to him while he missed being at home, at this striking moment in history.

As the pageantry unfolded in Westminster Abbey, I absorbed the passionate words by Diana's brother and soaked in Elton John's moving rendition of "Candle in the Wind." I also studied with a new interest the very Englishness of the event: the women's hats; the grandeur of the thousand-year-old building; the colourful uniforms certain men wore; the flowing robes of the bishops and clergy.

As it was a Saturday, I hadn't wanted to miss out on my aerobics class, so I excused myself from the debrief of the funeral and headed out to the gym. After my sweat fest, Nicholas and I grabbed a sandwich, and I was struck by how so many people started chatting to us when they heard his accent. Everyone wanted to talk about Diana and her untimely death, asking Nicholas how he was faring while being so far from home.

And now the afternoon stretched before me and I had plenty of time to give myself a manicure, shave my legs, and perfect my hair and makeup. It was a sad day of mourning the People's Princess, but I trusted the events of the evening would be those to remain in our memories.

At 6:30 pm I started to pace around the living room, looking out the window. I wondered, *"When's he going to get here? He's a half-hour late already. He's not usually late."*

Ten minutes later he drove up in his borrowed car. "Sorry I'm late," Nicholas said, looking flustered. "You look lovely."

"Thank you!" I said, giving him an air kiss to keep from messing up my lipstick. "I was getting worried. So where are we going?"

"You know I'm not going to tell you. It's a surprise!"

We got on the Beltway and headed towards the District.[1] He seemed anxious and didn't talk much. After a half hour or so, we made it to the lovely area in northwest DC near to where the Vice President lives, where the streets brim with magnificent mansions. It dawned on me that we were near Embassy Row and the British Embassy. I thought, *"Nice – he's going to propose on British soil!"*

But as we approached the embassy, traffic was congested. Police officers directed cars and entrepreneurs sold flowers. The place swarmed with people wanting to pay their respects to the fallen princess.

After fifteen minutes of circling the area, we finally found a place to park, several blocks from the embassy. Nicholas grabbed a dozen roses from the trunk[2] and took my hand, and after walking a block I was sorry that I had worn high heels.

Eventually we made it through the crowds to the burgeoning makeshift memorial. There we stood in silence in the twilight, surrounded by mourners who were lighting candles, saying prayers, and adding their flowers. I wondered what Nicholas was feeling, being here and not in England. As I gazed at the tributes and flowers, I thought about the beautiful woman whose life had ended so prematurely. About those two young boys who would grow up without her. About a life of privilege that sounded like it was wracked with pain. About the scenes of grief that had seemed to explode on the streets of London from the normally stiff-upper-lipped British people.

But my thoughts quickly returned to myself and my exciting relationship with this Englishman. After meeting at the book club, we had spent as much time together as we could for the few months while he was in Virginia before he returned to England for the end of the summer term at his theological college.[3] We had been apart over the summer, communicating by letter when he was on placement in South Africa and then again by phone and email when he returned to England, this being before the days of video chats. Finally we reunited when he came back to Virginia for a visit at the end of the summer. The death of Diana shortly after he arrived had shaped our time together as we listened to the unfolding news story with sadness.

Having talked about marriage for months – even completing our premarital counselling before getting engaged – I knew that he would propose during this trip. The months of waiting would be over and finally we could announce to our family and friends our intention to marry. I would also give my informal notice at work, for I knew that marrying Nicholas meant moving to England, at least for the first few years while he completed theological training and served his curacy.[4]

Standing before the piles of flowers for Diana, I mused about plans and dreams, flitting between the poignancy of her death and excitement about my life to come. Then suddenly I caught my breath as I watched Nicholas set his dozen roses on the memorial to Diana. Those were *my* roses! My heart started to race as I tried to figure out what he was doing, and why in the world he was giving my flowers to Diana.

Then he turned and reached for me, burying a sob. I embraced him back, somewhat stiffly while wondering what was happening.

Finally he said, "Let's go back to the car."

I nodded, flummoxed. I couldn't figure out what had just taken place, for I had been so sure that he intended to give *me* those flowers, not Diana. I prided myself on my intuition and now wondered how I had got things so wrong.

We stumbled through the rest of the night, with nothing seeming to go right. The restaurant in Old Town Alexandria where Nicholas had booked a table had released it when we were over an hour late. They seated us in a back room next to the clanging kitchen doors, waiters entering and exiting every ten seconds. With my nerves on edge, I couldn't bear the distractions and asked if we could find someplace else to eat. We walked around Old Town, my feet aching with every step, and finally found a restaurant that had a nice table for us outside. But our conversation was stilted, and eventually I clammed up, tired of trying to keep it going. I still held out hope that he'd pop the question but I was all jumbled up inside. Dessert came and went with no proposal in sight. After he paid the bill, Nicholas said, "Why don't we walk by the river?"

"Sounds great," I said, still wondering when he would propose.

Romance must have been in the air, for when we got to the river we couldn't find an empty bench anywhere. Couples dotted around the edge of the water in various stages of embrace. Finally we found somewhere to sit, but soon realized why the bench hadn't been occupied, for the nearby streetlamp illuminated our every move. I wondered what else could go wrong.

After twenty minutes of silence, Nicholas said, "Well, let's call it a night."

With his words, the realization hit me that he wasn't going to propose. I sucked in my breath, trying to keep my emotions in check, not wanting to let him see me cry while wondering what in the world he was thinking.

When I finally got home, I muffled my tears to keep from disturbing my roommate's[5] friend in the next room. I stemmed the sobs long enough to dial Kristen's number, hoping she'd answer. "He didn't propose," I choked out through the tears that I couldn't hold back.

"What? I can't believe it. What happened?"

As I told her about the events of the night, we were stumped. After hanging up, I cleaned my face of the makeup I had so carefully applied, aching with the unanswered questions and unfulfilled hopes. Getting into bed, I reached for my Bible, but the words didn't register. *"Why, Lord?"* I wondered.

I was numb the next morning as I climbed into Nicholas's car to go to church. He handed me a note and we drove in silence as I read it, stifling my tears. In it he said that he had lost his nerve while at the British Embassy. For while standing there in front of the makeshift memorial to Diana, he had felt the Lord say that in marrying me, at some point he might be away from his homeland, and was he willing to count the cost? As he considered this momentous decision, he realized he wasn't ready to move forward. But he was sorry.

"I don't know how to respond to this," I said, waving the note and biting my lip as he parked the car.

I somehow managed to hold back my tears throughout the tortuous service, but I couldn't concentrate on the prayers, hymns, or the sermon. When it was time for Holy Communion, I spotted my lovely septuagenarian friend Mary Matheson at the prayer rail. As I knelt, I burst into tears while trying to tell her what had happened.

"Come with me, dear," she said. She led me back to the choir room, where I heaved deep sobs while recounting my tale of woe. "I guess he isn't ready to get married," I choked out.

"I don't know what's going on with him," she said. "I'm so, so sorry." She held me as I cried, and after a while said, "Let me pray for you."

Her prayers brought some peace, and after a while I was able to pull myself together enough to face Nicholas and the other churchgoers. When the service ended, we made our way to his car and drove back to my house in silence.

When he pulled in the parking spot, I realized I had to tell him what I was feeling, for he had no idea just how much he had hurt me. I turned to him and said, "You are like a bull in the china shop of my heart. You have knocked over the crystal and have drawn blood."

To my surprise, Nicholas started crying. "I'm so sorry," he said. "I guess I'm just not ready. I need to work on being a man."

Before I knew what I was saying, I uttered, hoping he wouldn't agree, "Sounds like we need to call off the wedding."

"Yes, I think so."

I was stunned at how quickly everything was happening. One day I was planning my move to England with my new husband and the next we were ending our relationship. In disbelief I said, "Okay. Well, I'll cancel my trip to England too."

"I guess that's right," he said.

Pushing down emotion, I said, "I have a few things of yours. I'll get them together before you go back to England." I walked away from the car, struggling with my key in the lock. *"Lord,"* I prayed, *"What's going on? What about marriage and children and moving to England?"*

When I got into my room, on my own in the house, finally I was able to release the sobs I had been holding back most of the morning. I felt like I was living in an alternate reality, for nothing felt real. I called a friend who was a mentor figure, and she listened quietly as I laid out the sorry tale. Shortly after I hung up with her, the phone rang. *"I hardly want to answer it,"* I thought. *"What if it's Nicholas?"*

It was my friend Martha, wanting to know how I was. She said, "I could see you from the front of the church and you looked just so distressed. Is everything all right?"

The afternoon wore on with more phone calls, including to my mom and dad and several other friends. My parents were distraught for me, hearing my pain and trying to comfort me from a thousand miles away. Everyone seemed shocked at the sudden reversal. As I talked with my friend Cheryl, I asked her what I should do. "I can't call him, can I? He's the one who ended things."

"No, I wouldn't call him if I were you," she answered. "I think he needs to figure out what's going on in that head of his. But if he comes over, you can fling the door open!"

"That's a nice thought," I said. "Don't know if it will happen, but I can hope."

Spent from all of the discussing and crying, not to mention my broken dreams, I lay on the bed and stared at the ceiling, studying the dust in the light fixtures and the slight burn marks in the paint from the too-strong light bulbs. I thought, *"I guess I'll need to fix that up, now that I'm going to be here longer."*

When I heard the door above me open, marking the home-coming of one of my roommates, I hoped she wouldn't come downstairs, for I was zapped of energy. I listened to the footsteps move along the living room to the kitchen, and then later go up the stairs to the top floor of bedrooms. I was grateful to be left alone.

I wallowed in hurt and self-pity for another hour, and then suddenly heard the doorbell. I hardly dared to hope as I made my way upstairs to answer the door.

*"Fling the door open. Fling the door open,"* I thought. Before me stood Nicholas with a dozen red roses. He reached his arms out to embrace me, and I ran toward him. As he held me, he whispered, "I'm so very sorry. Can I come in?"

"Of course," I said, choking back tears of joy and disbelief.

When we got to my room, he closed the door and I sat on the bed, heart pounding and every nerve on edge. With a decisive motion, he took one of the roses, broke off the stem, and handed it to me. "Amy, will you do me the honour of being my wife?"

"I would love that," I said, laughing.

The proposal came a day later than I anticipated, but it came. Later Nicholas shared with me the stress and strife he'd suffered – not only his overwhelmed feeling at the British Embassy at the enormity of joining two lives together, but the things that went wrong leading up to our dinner as I preened and planned. He hadn't been able to connect with my parents, to ask my father for my hand in marriage; he tried to pick up the engagement ring but the store didn't have it ready; even booking the restaurant and getting the roses in a foreign country had proved challenging. For him, that strong sense of God's question while at the memorial for Diana proved to be the tipping point as he relinquished the idea of proposing that night. As I would learn as we melded our lives together, the narrative of events always has two points of view.

I didn't realize it at the time, but I can see now how many factors came together to deter Nicholas from proposing, and that he bottled it *because* he took the commitment so seriously. He's a quintessential Englishman, quirks and all, who loves his country. I thus had no idea how deep that prompting from God would go – how he had to ponder if he'd be willing to sacrifice even his beloved homeland if he united with me. The power of such a question added to the emotion of days of watching the news about Diana's death and feeling so removed from the scenes of heartbreak on the streets of Britain.

I had started the evening off so sure of how things would go. Had this been the days of social media, I probably would have posted a photo of me dressed up, saying, "Excited about the night; watch this space!" I had it all planned out, but I was wrong. Life, God, events, the world, people – stuff intervenes and changes our expectations. That failed marriage proposal knocked a bit off of my pride and my surety about things to come. Marriage would provide more smoothing of my rough edges as it would give me eyes to see – if I chose – just how sinful and stubborn I could be.

Only years after the proposal episode could I discern how cultural differences came into play during this pivotal moment in our relationship. To use generalized terms, I was the optimistic "let's get this show on the road" person by culture and temperament while he held the "we need to stop and think this through and not rattle the system" approach. I see now the richness of blending two cultures coming together – the mother country and the rebellious child – even if at times the differences require dollops of communication, understanding, and grace. Five months after Diana's funeral, I married Nicholas and moved to England. The place that had just been an image on a screen was now my home. I was about to step into the answer to a burning question: What happens when dreams become reality? How do two people meld their lives together?

# 3

# SCHOOL DAYS

New Year's Day may be all about new starts, resolutions, and recovery, but in practice the new year begins at the start of September. Summer has waned and the nights turn nippy. Holidays[1] fade into our memories as kids go back to school and work and church resumes. A new preaching series starts and gym classes get crowded again. It's time to dig in to new challenges and responsibilities.

When I was single, September was my annual vacation time. My friends and I would drive down the East Coast to the Outer Banks of North Carolina to dine on crabs, soak up the sun, and play in the surf. Rollerblading, late nights giggling and dreaming, walks in and among the waves, chatting to surfer dudes – life was blissful.

September holidays now are a thing of the past as we're locked into school schedules, at the mercy of high air fares. Now in September the realization of the coming cold weather hits me as I wonder how long before the vicarage renders me a shivering mass of chills, swathed in wool and fleece. But I love the return to routine. I adore my kids, yet I welcome the first Monday morning when the Pyelets go back to school and I'm basking in my sunny study, with no one needing me or clamouring for my attention.

Never would I have anticipated I'd have children growing up in the English school system, but we live a life of surprises. Key stage 1 – huh? GCSEs and A levels? School uniforms? Summers only six weeks long, instead of three months? I didn't like uniforms at first, but I've been won over by the ease of my daughter's only choices being skirt, trousers, or dress. In terms of the approach to education, I'm learning the benefits and challenges of a system different from what I grew up with. Such as the depth that zeroing down to a few subjects can impart as the children grow and move up the educational system, rather than the broad approach more favoured in the States, with many students entering university not yet knowing what liberal arts subjects they'll major in. Being a generalist serves my kind of brain well, but not those whose minds hold a scary amount of detailed information, like Nicholas and Joshua. For them, a deep grasp of subjects such as history fuels their passion and sets them alive.

One thing I'm sorry my children miss out on, living on this side of the Atlantic, is riding the yellow school bus. It's verily a rite in the States, a cushion to the day that signals the beginning and end to the formal learning sessions, which also provides an important time for socialization.

Growing up, my siblings and I lived on the edge geographically of taking the bus to school or getting there by foot. Walking there was just a bit too far in the frigid Minnesota winters, so we opted to ride the bus. Joining at the first stop, we had the choice of seats, moving from the front of the bus to the back as we grew in years and levels of cool. Friendships were strengthened – or not – on the bus, and sometimes homework was hurriedly completed. In junior high, I used the time to apply or remove my forbidden makeup. But for my kids, Joshua and Jessica, the big yellow school bus will be something only out of the movies.

Yet we have the school run, and I love that we can get to school and back on foot, not having to drive but building exercise into our day. When the Pyelets were very young, we had a series of German au pairs, and I delegated the morning school run to them.[2] But when Jessica started school full time, we said goodbye to our last German au pair and I inherited the school run.

Getting ready for school, and then making the journey there, can be rife with stress. Lollygagging children, dragging their feet. Misplaced bits of uniform. Gary-the-Caretaker ringing the bell at the gate, signalling its imminent closure. Tears and meltdowns and stress – and that's just the parents. In the autumn of Jessica being in year two,[3] one morning she decided, in a flash, that she had outgrown her princess scooter. Her friends, she informed me, would now make fun of her and her "babyish" scooter. On the same day, Joshua, who prizes autonomy, spiralled downward when he was informed that yes, on this rainy day he had to wear a coat. I wasn't loving life. Halfway along our mile walk to school, with many tears shed because of the now-offensive scooter, Jessica stepped in some dog poo. Then she scooted through a massive puddle, getting soaked in the process. Stinky poo and soggy shoes and trousers; the morning wasn't getting any better. Joshua, who despises being late, cranked at her for holding us up.

I'm afraid I uttered words I shouldn't have in a tone of voice that was not conducive to good parenting. Soon after my outburst, I regretted my actions and asked my kids to forgive me, which they did. Joshua said farewell with a smile at our approved place, eager to go the rest of the way on his own. And Jessica wasn't too old yet for me to give her a huge hug at the school gate and to whisper a prayer in her ear. Gary had only started to ring the bell.

I lost it on that occasion, and that's not the only time I've not been a perfect parent. But more days than not, the kids and I have interesting and fun conversations on the way to and from school. "Tell me about your childhood," says Jessica. "Besides Barbies, what was your favourite toy?" The afternoon school run is an important time to me to hear about their days – if other pupils are being difficult; what happened on the football field; how they did in their spelling test. They might miss out on the yellow school bus, but the school run is pretty great too. But not so much when it's raining.

And yes, I'm the only parent whizzing to the school gate on a bright green scooter.

The school gate. Oh my, the school gate.

I had no idea about the school gate when our au pairs would deposit our children at school. Then it was my turn, and I started to stress. I got up early and applied makeup and chose my clothes with care. After all, I had appearances to fret over and yummy mummies to compare myself with.

My sister, an ocean away, asked, "Why don't you just wear your workout clothes?"

I had a hard time explaining how that didn't feel proper. I thought to myself, *"Proper, proper; everything must be proper over here!"*

Feeling the need to dress up more than in jeans and a sweat-shirt, I'd wait at the school gate for the Pyelets to exit from their classrooms. "When did I return to high school?" I'd wonder as I nervously eyed up the groups of mothers chatting. There are the popular ones, I'd think; there's a group who've just had coffee together; there's the group from Japan; there's the parent who has moved her older children to the posh public school nearby.

Sometimes I'd hear whispers, such as the time I complained about the school's parent group hosting a night at the races to raise money. "This is a Church of England school," I had said. "Why do we want to support gambling?" When I walked past a group of women, I heard wafts of, "She's the American who . . ."

But after a few years, I made a conscious decision not to mind any imagined or real cliques. Instead of looking long-ingly at the group of yummy mummies, I'd search out the woman on her own, standing forlornly, and strike up a con-versation. Or I'd chat with the yummies – and realize that I shouldn't resort to cheap generalizations.

One thing I adore about our kids' primary school[4] is the make-up of its members. We have representatives from every continent, diversity that makes for richness. I love how my kids can pronounce any non-Anglo-Saxon name without trouble; how they can detect the difference in pronunciation when I fail to say things correctly. How when I describe some-one, Jessica will say, "What colour is her hair? What colour is her skin?" Diversity here is normal, and a little taste of heaven.

My days of the school run are waning, however, as Joshua moves to secondary school.[5] Yes, independent travelling – the term that strikes fear into the heart of parents. We're slowly letting him make the journey on his own, which he loves, but images of mangled flesh flash before my eyes as I imagine the things that could happen.

One morning I got a frantic phone call from him after I had just passed him on his way to school as I walked back home from dropping off Jessica to early-morning choir.

"Mom! My scooter broke!"

"Are you okay?" I asked.

"I'm not sure."

I turned around at a fast clip, making my way back to him, heart pounding for more reasons than the unexpected run. When I found him he was standing on the pavement[6] with a look of disbelief. I hugged him, relieved that he wasn't bruised and broken. I was aghast to see his scooter though, for the upright bar had split off from the base, even though the contraption was only a couple of months old. A bad piece of engineering.

I gave thanks to the Lord, grateful that my son hadn't been hurt. I reflected on how I always try to breathe a prayer for him when he goes on his own, but how after I had greeted him in passing, he had stayed on my mind and I prayed for him with a sense of surprising urgency.

Regarding kids who travel to school on their own, I'm fascinated by different cultural approaches. I threw the question out on a social media site, asking, "Would you let your 10- or 11-year-old walk a mile to school on his/her own? From my British friends, no outright "no's," but from my American friends, many, including: "No. Too paranoid. Could not live with myself if something happened." I resonate with that, but more so with another American's response: "Where we live in England? Yes. In America? No, and in part because of the judgemental attitude of other parents." A couple of times when Americans have visited, they've been surprised at the measures of independence our kids have on the roads, such as me letting my then 8-year-old son make his way home from the park across the busy street.

Part of the difference has to do with the sheer size of America compared with the UK and the predominance of the car in that big country, but this applies to rural areas of Britain as well – how can kids safely walk along grassy verges with lorries[7] barrelling down the road? As an American friend said, "Where we live there are no sidewalks. Traffic is too fast; it's barely friendly to bicyclists. Truly urban areas would be better suited."

But the discussion revealed a cultural difference that partly made me smile, and partly made me take pause. One Yankee friend jokingly suggested he'd only allow his child walk to school if they could carry a gun (a "concealed carry," as it's known), and another piped in, tongue-in-cheek, wondering where the child would store the weapon at school. The very suggestion of kids and guns horrified some of my British friends who, not surprisingly, missed the joking banter as the whole discussion fell outside of their usual conversational categories.

I've changed course on this loaded issue through my years in the UK. When Stateside I used to date a guy who would take me shooting and I could see the point of the right to bear arms, deeply rooted in the US Constitution and the very identity of this independent frontier nation. But now I can't comprehend why this superpower can't pass and uphold a few laws to stop the madness. Columbine, Sandy Hook, too many others to list – the killing of kids continues and my heart breaks.

This cultural difference came back to me vividly when I was video chatting with my goddaughter and her mother. When I asked how I could be praying for her, one response related to her fear emanating out of the school lock-down practice drills. Growing up in Minnesota, we had regular tornado drills where we'd crouch in hallways to avoid the potential of shattering glass thrown by the high winds. But drills against shooters? I have no categories.

I'm aware I'm making deeply unpopular statements to many Americans. For instance, I recently met one living in Britain who told me about the blind gun training she received the last time she was Stateside. She remarked, "If you're going to need to defend yourself, you need to be able to shoot in the dark."

Another difference between our two cultures lies in attitudes to faith in schools; I've taken years to wrap my head around government-sponsored schools that have roots in faith. It just doesn't happen in the States – the separation of church and state is deeply embedded in the US Constitution (well, the First Amendment), so never shall a US public school host a nativity play nor say the Lord's Prayer at the end of an assembly. I suppose I should hold firm views about which educational system is better, but like healthcare, I can see pros and cons of each.

On the cons side of the UK approach is the danger of the Christian faith being marginalized or taken for granted – for it to be seen as just part of the furniture. God belongs in chapel, and nowhere else, or so the received wisdom goes. The nativity play morphs from a grand enactment of a vital part of the Christian faith to merely a sweet story of a young couple searching for a place to have their first child. It becomes a seasonal event at which to coo over our adorable offspring, dressed up in their tea towels and animal costumes, with the vaunted roles of Mary and Joseph secretly fought over by pushy parents. One night at book club I exclaimed my glee at Jessica being named Mary, but then looked around the room and realized, to my horror, that four other women there had daughters in her year group. Open mouth; insert foot.

I don't want God shoved into a box, only to come out for the cursory prayer at the end of the school assembly. Nor do I want pupils forced to pray if they don't believe – I know many children in church schools follow different faiths or none. But my kids delight in their religious education lessons. Both of them love sharing their knowledge of the Christian faith, and Joshua more often than not volunteers to write the concluding prayer when his class leads an assembly. The wonder of my American friends at a government school actually putting on a nativity play makes me stop to consider, for the US system has moved completely the opposite way in eradicating any kind of faith practice. Does that mean that a sort of *de facto* secular humanism reigns?

And I have to admit that we gain lovely people at our church through their regular attendance when they want that all-important vicar's signature on the admission form for church schools. Our Church of England secondary school has only been around for five or six years, but already has received two votes of confidence from Ofsted – outstanding.[8] And so parents have a good incentive to come to our church twice a month for two years – their child is nearly guaranteed one of the 180 places (with 1,100 applicants last year).

Some parents feel forced to go to church in order for their children to get into good schools, and some clergy are scathing about ulterior motives for church attendance. But which of us ever has pure motives?

> School days, school days
> Dear old golden rule days . . .

Oh, sorry, my British friends – you won't know that old American ditty. How about we move next to a holiday I knew little about before moving here; one that celebrates the sacrifice of those willing to lose themselves that others might find themselves.

# 4

# "WE WILL REMEMBER"

I write on Remembrance Day, during the year that marks the hundred-year anniversary of the start of the First World War. The so-called "war to end all wars." The war that claimed nearly 900,000 lives from people in the Commonwealth. The war that America only entered in 1917.

The amazing art installation at the Tower of London in 2014 captured the hearts of millions with its handmade ceramic poppy planted for each of those lives lost. We went to visit the Tower on that Remembrance Sunday – we and a few thousand others. Though we only gazed at the sea of red for a short time, jostled by the crowds, the sight moved us. Not least because 152 of those poppies stood for men whose names appear on the two war memorials in our church.

Nicholas and Joshua, lovers of history both, dug up information about these men on the memorials, scouring websites about ancestry and that of the Commonwealth War Graves Commission for clues. What were the backgrounds and interests of these men? How did they die? Our intrepid researchers even took a field trip to the London Metropolitan Archives to search out the original church documents and revel in such items as the 1920 invoice for our church's north transept stained-glass window, entitled "Saints in Glory," installed to commemorate the fallen soldiers, sailors, and airmen.

On Remembrance Sunday, a group of people young and old read out the 152 names, while members of the congregation placed a poppy for each person at the foot of the cross. Direct descendants of the men on the memorial were invited to the service – some came from Sussex, Kent, and even Australia – as well as the occupants of the homes where the men lived before going to war.

All this research brought home the personal nature of the sacrifice of these men. No longer were they just statistics of those who died, but fathers, brothers, sons, husbands; writers and bricklayers, police constables and trainee architects, dentists and regulars in the military; two men who died in the same German prison camp; at least three sets of brothers. The youngest man was aged 17, the eldest 48.

I knew little about Remembrance Day – or Armistice Day – before coming to the UK. We celebrate Veteran's Day on 11 November in the States, but although it's a public holiday, it's not one that captures the imagination of the nation. That honour goes to Memorial Day, celebrated the fourth Monday in May. Americans (including me) often confuse or don't know the difference between the two: Veteran's Day celebrates the service of all US military veterans, while Memorial Day commemorates those who died while serving.

Why do Americans prefer Memorial Day over Veteran's Day? A friend suggested it might be because it falls on a Monday in summer, making it a long weekend, and "We don't need another November holiday." She's onto something there; Thanksgiving was well established before Armistice Day came about at the end of World War I.

Another reason lies in what Memorial Day used to be called – Decoration Day, named for the decorating of graves as the holiday emerged from the American Civil War in the late 1860s. With so many soldiers dying on both sides of the conflict, mourners had a plethora of graves on which to place a wreath or flowers. Relatives would travel great distances, meeting together to remember their loved ones with some solemn moments, perhaps joining in some gospel songs, as well as having more lighthearted times of picnicking and playing games together.

So when living Stateside, for me not only was Veteran's Day one of those less-celebrated holidays that only federal employees would get off from work, but war – even the Second World War – seemed a lifetime away. The only connection I thought I had was a great uncle from California who saw military action in Europe, which he never mentioned. My mom told us about his service when we visited the American cemetery in Cambridge.

But in the writing of this book, I learned about another relative who died in the war. When my dad read a draft copy of the manuscript, he told me the story of his uncle Harold, his mom's younger brother. When my dad was about 5 years old, his mom answered the phone and suddenly started to weep like he had never seen before, for she learned that Harold had died in Italy. Another of her brothers served as well, and, according to my dad, "always held a bit of a grudge against General Patton, under whom Harold served." War reaches farther than I realized.

On this side of the Atlantic, many people still hold vivid memories of the Second World War, my in-laws included. They were children then, my father-in-law upended from his family in southeast London and sent to the countryside for safety. Living on a farm meant he accessed more food than he would have in London, but he was far from his parents and two of his siblings, though one sister was housed with a family near to him.

My mother-in-law's family, in east London, wondered what the safest approach would be, and considered sending the children to Canada. But when a German submarine sunk a boat filled with British children bound for that land, they decided if they were going to die, they would die together, and stayed put for the duration. My mother-in-law still feels chills when she hears a recording of a doodlebug (the V-1 flying bomb). During the peak of the German usage of this device in 1944, more than a hundred a day were fired at southeast England.

I've learned about both world wars from living here, not least being married to a historian who loves modern history. For the first part of our French honeymoon, we toured some battlefields in the Somme and visited military museums. (We later toured the fabulous Moët & Chandon wine cellars in Epernay before heading south to the hairpin turns and breathtaking views of the Gorges du Tarn.) We also went to some of the cemeteries housing whole cohorts of men from, say, Devon or Dorset, in what were known as the pals' battalions. Lord Kitchener, seeking ways to encourage men to sign up for the First World War, came up with the idea, thinking that the camaraderie of serving with one's mates would draw more men to enlist. He didn't anticipate how villages and towns would be rocked when these battalions suffered casualties, though, and the units were soon eradicated.

Some years after our honeymoon we visited Omaha Beach, sitting not far from the sword-like memorial. We enjoyed our picnic on the beach, soaking in the French sunshine and watching Joshua play in the sand, when the peaceful scene was interrupted by a busload of jostling French students. Nicholas remarked, "You know, it's probably because of your ancestors fighting right here that those schoolchildren are free. And speaking French today." I reflected and gave thanks for those who gave their lives that we might be free.

The first time I heard about Remembrance Sunday, I was dating Nicholas, back when his Englishness seemed exotic and other. One of his assignments was to preach a sermon to the class that was videoed and then pulled apart and analyzed by the students and teacher. When he showed me the video with his Remembrance Sunday sermon, I started to realize how much I didn't know about him or his home country, such as how much the world wars had affected it.

Remembrance Sunday continues to be one of Nicholas's favourite services to take, for it marries his passion for history with his love of liturgy and worship. He organizes members of the congregation to take part, asking our oldest member to read from the Act of Remembrance the moving lines, "They shall grow not old as we who are left grow old. Age shall not weary them, nor the years condemn." A young person reads in response, "At the going down of the sun, and in the morning, we will remember them."

Last year Nicholas shared the moving story of Billy MacFadzean, a soldier from Belfast who signed up with the

Ulster Volunteers but never came home. He died on the morning of the first day of the Battle of the Somme, receiving the Victoria Cross posthumously. He was standing next to one of the trenches, near to a soldier opening a box of bombs before an attack. The box slid down into the trench, which was crowded with men, and two of the safety pins fell out. Billy realized the danger and threw himself on top of the bombs, which exploded, killing him but only injuring one other.[1]

As Nicholas said, "He gave himself for his friends. Seeing the danger, he willingly sacrificed his life for them. But what Jesus has done is even more incredible. Billy died for his friends, but Jesus died for his enemies. As Romans 5:8 says, 'But God demonstrates his own love for us in this: while we were still sinners, Christ died for us.'"

The two world wars were filled with soldiers who fought and sometimes died in the quest for freedom: scholars and poets, plumbers and mechanics, pilots and chefs and businessmen. For these heroes of the past and the country in whose name they served, I am truly grateful. We will remember.

# 5

# BRINGING IN THE SHEAVES

**A Special Prayer for [American] Thanksgiving**
Almighty and gracious Father, we give you thanks for the fruits of the earth in their season and for the labors of those who Harvest them. Make us, we pray, faithful stewards of your great bounty, thankful for the provision of our necessities and supportive of the relief of all who are in need, to the glory of your Name; through Jesus Christ our Lord, who lives and reigns with you and the Holy Spirit, one God, now and forever. Amen.[1]

We arrived at Winfield House, the London residence of the US ambassador, with me a flutter of nerves. It was my third Thanksgiving in this country, and to my astonishment, Nicholas and I received a last-minute invitation to the official Thanksgiving feast at this stately house. I had researched the list of others attending – an intimate gathering of fifty – my anxiety rising as I glimpsed the names of novelists, business leaders, members of the arts and media, and other high-ranking individuals with whom we'd share the meal.

During the cocktail hour, two gentlemen meandered over to us and we started talking. I knew from his distinctive looks that one of them was Andrew Lloyd Webber, but I wasn't sure about the other. Someone important, no doubt, as they chatted about their ladies (as in Lords and Ladies) being at home for the night. Later I asked Nicholas if that man was David Frost. "Yes," he said, "Sir David, you mean."

At that time I worked for one of the large publishing conglomerates as a commissioning[2] editor for their religious books. Through connections with friends in the States, I knew the US ambassador at the time, so my boss and I had met up with him at Winfield House one morning in early November to discuss potential book ideas. I was in awe at the grandeur of the ambassador's residence, which he told us had been sold to the American government for one dollar by Barbara Hutton, the daughter of the man who created Woolworth's.

When I received the invitation on the day before Thanksgiving, I was struck by the formal wording, such as "Carriages at 10:30 pm." I also wondered what they meant by "lounge suits" in terms of dress, so in a panic I asked Nicholas to accompany me shopping to try to find something suitable. The women were more dressed up than I realized they would be; in hindsight, I didn't need to buy a business suit but should have worn a dress.

Nicholas, the only clergyperson there, gave the grace before the meal – with the ambassador asking him a couple of minutes before we went through to the dining area. His prayer was the right length – not too long – and audible, and I was proud of him. I managed the dinner conversation without the comfort of Nicholas next to me, for he was seated across the room. I enjoyed having one of the ambassador's daughters at my table though, asking her about life in the UK compared with her school and activities in the States.

During the evening, we met the man who had been the British ambassador in Washington, DC, at the time of Nicholas's ill-fated marriage proposal. We recounted a little of his attempt, saying how put off he had been by the flower sellers and people mourning Diana's death. The former ambassador said, "Ah, had I known, we would have invited you in for a drink and you could have proposed inside!"

As the evening ended our carriage came (albeit the "hackney"[3] rather than the horse-drawn variety) and we drove off to the Tube station. I was humbled to have been invited but also relieved that this memorable experience was over. And I wished that they wouldn't have put marshmallows on the sweet potatoes.[4]

Later I learned that the ambassador had invited me to be a link to home for his daughter, for I had connections to a family friend. I conveyed this explanation to my boss, the publishing director, whom I suspect was glad to know what was behind the puzzling invitation of a lowly commissioning editor. He, a high-flyer, would have felt eminently more at home at the dinner than I.

I have to admit that for a long time I didn't realize that the British celebration of Harvest underpins the American celebration of Thanksgiving. The Pilgrim fathers and mothers observed days of fasting and days of feasting, one of the latter at Harvest, through which the modern Thanksgiving holiday was born.

Devout in their faith, the Pilgrims left England in 1608 for Amsterdam in search of religious freedom. They lived there twelve years before the foreign culture wore them down and they decided to head for the New World. Their journey on the Mayflower, however, was desperate. The ship they travelled on was designed to carry cargo, not passengers. And the cabin where they slept was intended for thirty people, not eighty. Their food rotted and became infested with insects; they nearly drowned when the ship's main beam cracked; they endured ridicule from the sailors. They pressed on through their five-month journey across the Atlantic – though admittedly they didn't have much choice.

When they arrived in what is now Massachusetts, the Pilgrims faced a new set of challenges: a new land called for the planting of food and the building of places to live. But in all things they gave thanks, observing a full day of Sabbath each week. After surviving their first harsh winter, they hosted a three-day feast that we now name as the first Thanksgiving. During this celebration, they gave thanks for their food, for seven houses built, for a peace treaty with the Native Americans, and most importantly for the freedom to worship God. The women cooked, the men played games, and they all shared stories and returned thanks to the Lord. They invited the Native Americans who helped them acclimatize to this strange new world to join them at their table.

This is the account I've always heard, but lately some contest it. I've learned that we base this vaunted holiday on what might be a lot of lore, for we only have a 115-word account from that first Thanksgiving. The pilgrim Edward Winslow wrote a letter to England after the feast, including this brief description (and note the "u" in *labours* hadn't got lost yet):

> Our Harvest being gotten in, our Governor sent four men on fowling; that so we might, after a more special manner, rejoice together, after we had gathered the fruit of our labours. They four, in one day, killed as much fowl as, with a little help besides, served the Company almost a week. At which time, amongst other recreations, we exercised our Arms; many of the Indians coming amongst us. And amongst the rest, their greatest King, Massasoyt, with some ninety men; whom, for three days, we entertained and feasted. And they went out, and killed five deer: which they brought to the Plantation; and bestowed on our Governor, and upon the Captain, and others.[5]

Slim historical evidence notwithstanding, the tradition grew, if not every year at first. And probably turkey wasn't the centrepiece during that first celebration, but goose or duck. Later during the Revolutionary War, George Washington and his army stopped on their way to Valley Forge in bitter weather to mark the occasion. The practice then became solidified when in 1863 President Abraham Lincoln declared that the last Thursday in November would be a national day of Thanksgiving. Then in 1941 a joint resolution of both houses of Congress decreed, and President Franklin Delano Roosevelt signed into law, the bill establishing that the fourth Thursday of November shall now and always be Thanksgiving.

For me, celebrating US holidays while living in Britain can be poignant – Thanksgiving in particular. I work hard to create memories for our children of a taste of America, but the joy of celebrating comes with a corresponding ache as we're away from family and friends. I feel the loss of feasting with my countrypeople around a table heaving with turkey, stuffing, and gravy and of enjoying the friendship and lively conversation that ensues. Or, if I can admit it, being always-the-host, never-the-guest. Perhaps this longing hearkens to a deeper emotion we all experience – the longing for home.

I know that for many people on either side of the Atlantic, or further afield, holidays such as Thanksgiving don't hold the glossy-magazine image of loving family and friends surrounding a table bursting with food. They might enjoy material abundance but suffer emotional scarcity. Their feelings of loneliness and sadness might intensify as they think about how they are "supposed" to feel on special days of celebration. Glimpsing the chair that a loved one should occupy, but which now sits empty, breaks their hearts. Sitting bleakly at a half-empty table reminds them of the raging family feud. A loss of job weighs on their heart and mind.

Such situations can make it difficult to be thankful. And yet God can help us to give thanks and find peace even in the darkest of circumstances. For some people this will be harder than for others. A friend of mine, for instance, oozes seemingly relentless optimism. She might face surgery, but afterwards gives thanks for the medical team and her first meal – after three days of not eating – of mashed potato. Others struggle to see things for which they can give thanks when everything seems to herald gloom and doom and despair. Just finding a flicker of light to brighten the way challenges them. But for either personality, and those in between, if we can park our emotions and with our wills ask God to help us give thanks, he will answer that plea. We feel a glimmer of hope; we experience a rush of love; we are overcome with peace. Even a small seed of hope bears fruit.

Each year as I celebrate, yet with longings, I give thanks for my British friends who go out of their way to wish me a happy Thanksgiving. My social media networks burst with lovely sentiments, even though sometimes they also drip with the only-in-Britain humour. As the US ambassador recounted at the Thanksgiving service in 2014, a British friend said to him, "Don't worry. We celebrate July 4th here too. Only we call it Thanksgiving."[6]

Living in London, we enjoy attending the service at St Paul's Cathedral every year for Thanksgiving, in which some American clergy take part and the US ambassador delivers a message from the President. I never fail to be moved at the American anthem ringing through the hallowed English walls as servicemen march the US flag up to the front of the cathedral. The service, a highlight of the day, forms the backbone of our celebrations.

Joshua and Jessica delight in missing school for the day. We roast a turkey and, after many years, I've perfected my take on my mom's stuffing, adding dried cranberries – see the recipes at the end. One year a guest brought the mashed potatoes, not realizing just how much is needed to feed twelve guests. We had enough other food to keep us happy though – Minnesota wild rice, sweet potatoes (made with dried apricots; never with marshmallow on top), green beans . . . But that year I longed for a bigger repository for gravy (which an English friend revolutionized one year when she recommended adding a teaspoon of Marmite for more flavour).[7] And for dessert, I serve a pumpkin pie that even the natives enjoy – the secret is adding ice cream to the pumpkin puree, which softens the otherwise unfamiliar taste.[8]

Nicholas has shaped a Thanksgiving liturgy that we say together between courses (from which I took the prayers at the beginning and end of this chapter), employing American spellings to please me. The origins of the holiday may be rooted in escape from persecution in this country, but wherever we live, we can all be united in coming together to give thanks. After all, we're pilgrims in this life together.

For several years we've not hosted a big feast but have gone out to eat at a restaurant instead. Although enjoying someone else's labour of sourcing and cooking the food has its obvious benefits, the downside is the lack of the friends and family gathered around the table, joining together in a homey feast with laughter and rich conversation. And the regional variations of Thanksgiving come into focus, for restaurants may make the stuffing in an unrecognizable fashion or not serve up a green-bean casserole.

One of our most memorable Thanksgivings in Britain was that shared with one of my dearest friends from the Washington, DC area. Kathy added her regional flair by arranging for our feast a plate of crudités, in honour of her beloved mother, who had died decades before. Our long weekend was filled with experiences: she and I took tea in a posh London hotel; she treated Joshua to his first Chelsea match; she took Jessica to her first manicure; she listened to Nicholas's insider's tour of St Paul's Cathedral. Her comments as she left for the airport remain in my heart: "This was the best Thanksgiving ever."

In the last decade, US retailers have tacked on a new holiday to Thanksgiving – Black Friday, the biggest shopping day of the year for Yanks. Sadly, it seems to have made its way to these shores, ushered in by superstores and online giant Amazon. Why has Britain adopted this crazed consumeristic frenzy, but not the holiday in which to give thanks for the huge number of blessings we enjoy? I'm saddened by reports of mad scenes at supermarkets in the UK, such as in 2014 in Manchester when a flat-screen television fell on a woman in a wheelchair and another woman broke her wrist.

It beggars belief,[9] but people have even died from the madness that surrounds shoppers desperate to bag a deal. For instance, in 2008, an employee of Walmart was trampled to death in an out-of-control stampede in Long Island, New York. Even the people giving him CPR were pushed out of the way in the mad rush to buy discounted televisions and appliances. A website counts the total number of fatalities and injuries of Black Friday, which in 2021 reached 17 deaths and 125 injuries.[10] Black Friday indeed.

In case you were wondering, they named it Black Friday because it marks the start of the Christmas shopping season, when stores with the day's booming sales can get out of the red as they make a profit – thus going into the black. But as a friend said, "Black Friday is just another sign of the Americanization of our culture. We should at least call it by its traditional English name, St Primark's."[11]

If Britain adopts an American export, so much better would it be to reclaim its Harvest festival with a deepened emphasis on giving thanks. Yet in many parts of the country, Harvest remains an important celebration, one of the big festivals that even people who don't regularly attend church will join in with. Many churches host Harvest suppers and dances, including a ceilidh, which was a new concept to me, but when

I learned it was a Gaelic (Scottish/Irish) barn dance, I soon figured out what they were talking about. Other churches invite farmers to their services so that they can share how things are going for them, including what is working well and what is challenging.

People often bring their produce to church to give to those in need, which is then distributed through food banks and charities. In the past, the church would distribute the food locally, or other community-based organizations would take over this task. But now, with fewer people not in paid employment, churches and other organizations lack the vast volunteer force they used to have.

Many churches welcome these contributions, whether of tinned[12] goods and toiletries for food banks and homeless shelters, or the fresh produce from farmers which they may auction off the next day. As a friend remarked, thinking back to her younger years, "I remember it was mainly fresh foods that were brought, and they were sold off afterwards. It struck me as odd that we donated food and then bought it back, especially as, in our case, we had very little money."

Too much of a good thing can be a bad thing. One community in Jersey heard from the elderly residents who received bags and bags of fresh fruit and vegetables – both from the church and school celebrations – that they simply couldn't eat it all, and that it was rotting. "Besides," they said, "without wanting to sound ungrateful – we can afford to buy our own food."

One friend, when thinking about Harvest celebrations, said, "People bring food and we give it to the local homeless shelter. And sing anodyne songs about cabbages." Indeed, finding modern songs for Harvest can be a challenge for those leading the services. People love the old favourites, but they can feel dated. Yet as a friend said, "I used to love the hymns we sang at school for Harvest: 'We Plough the Fields and Scatter' and 'Come, Ye Thankful People, Come.' We weren't churchgoers and I think the services and assemblies were more special to me because of that."

Churches in urban areas often seek to tailor Harvest celebrations to their communities, for instance by exploring a theology of work. A friend recounted such a story from thirty years ago, which his dad told him. They lived in Derby, that industrial city most famous for its engineering work, with British Rail and Rolls Royce significant employers there. Their church wanted to reflect this heritage over the rather less relevant harvest from the fields. So they asked for people to contribute to the Harvest celebration from their working environment for an alternative display.

One member of the church worked at Rolls Royce and offered to bring in a jet engine as a focus. As my friend said, it couldn't have been one of the huge ones – not least because they require major machinery to move – but a small one, or perhaps parts of an engine. The engine made an impact, with church members gathering around and seeing it for the feat of engineering that it is. And they realized the difference this church member made at his place of work, transforming his patch with grace, truth, and light.

Only after the service, when the jet engine was removed, did the minister learn that the piece of machinery was worth over a million pounds – far more than the church building in the currency of those days. As my friend said, reflecting on the story, "It always makes me think that we should celebrate people's real harvest, and that we should be aware that some people's working lives are very different from what we might expect."[13]

Whether we celebrate Thanksgiving or Harvest, I like the idea of author Marion Stroud: "Why don't we, though, think in spiritual terms about the church and the harvest, in terms of what we've seen God bring to fruition and what seeds we want to plant in the coming year?"[14] Indeed – why not? The spiritual harvest, after all, seems to be the most important one.

For now is the time to plough up our ground and sow the seeds of righteousness, that we might reap the fruit of unfailing love as we seek the Lord until he comes and showers his goodness on us.[15]

### A Prayer for Grateful Hearts
Heavenly Father, giver of all things:
make us more thankful for what we have received,
make us more content with what we have,
make us more mindful of people in need,
and make us more ready to help and serve them in whatever
way we can,
as servants of Jesus Christ our Lord. Amen.[16]

And so the autumn leaves move from vibrant to withered, and as we head towards winter, no longer are the trees clothed, but bare. The days become shorter and nights longer, and we yearn for light. During these dark days we celebrate the Light that has come into the world, bringing hope, cheer, and new life.

# PART 2

# WINTER WONDERLAND

# 6

# LIFE AS A VW

"What a good vicar's wife you'll make!" So said the church-warden of the church where Nicholas would serve his curacy as she surveyed the heaving buffet table. Married and living in the UK just eight months, I was hosting a celebratory meal for Nicholas at his sending parish after his ordination as deacon in the Church of England. (Jargon alert – in the C of E, people are ordained deacon first, and then priest a year later.) I was new to the country and had made a range of salads, back when salads in Britain often consisted of browning iceberg lettuce, a few tomatoes, and salad cream. My raw-broccoli-streaky-bacon-grape salad was probably an anomaly, but I was so fresh to these shores that I didn't realize that it might appear exotic.

But how I cringed at her words. I had hosted the party as a gift of love for my husband as he moved into his new role, not out of duty or the need to embrace a label of a vicar's-wife-in-training. As I smiled and thanked her, I wondered why she had misunderstood my motives.

It was my first inkling that some people hold expectations for this animal that is a vicar's wife, or a VW as I like to say, which are often rooted in history. I had seen pastors' wives of all descriptions in the States, not taking much notice of them, not least as I grew up in the Roman Catholic tradition. But I was starting to gather that in the UK the caricature of a vicar's wife was either a behind-the-scenes power-wielding battle-axe or a kindly grandmother figure who made the tea and served the biscuits. And ran the children's rota and decorated the church and, and, and . . .

Yet I heard of women bucking the sometimes-constraining label too as they refused to bow to the expectations of others but stood tall in their identity, made in the image of God and created with their own callings and gifts. Perhaps that calling was to serve primarily in the church, but perhaps not.

I knew, for instance, a fellow American who had also married a Church of England minister. Their congregation embraced her and her role as a university lecturer, but I wonder if they raised their eyebrows at her flair and indomitable spirit, which she hinted at during her husband's induction service. Walking down the aisle at the end of the service, she flashed the T-shirt hitherto hidden under her respectable blazer, emblazoned with: "I don't bake cakes."

When Nicholas had been a curate in the Home Counties[1] for a few months, I crashed into unspoken expectations again. One Sunday morning, during the refreshment time in the slightly mildewy church hall, one of the older women said, "We're so delighted to welcome you on Tuesday, Amy!"

"Sorry, Tuesday?" I asked.

"Yes, to the over fifties club."

"Oh, Nicholas must be joining you then; I didn't know. I'm sorry, but I work in London during the week, and I'm not able to come."

She was a widowed vicar's wife in her eighties, and had been a teacher before she married. At that time, the vicar's wife was expected to give up any paid employment so that she could work alongside her husband in the parish. This woman had done so willingly, feeling it part of God's call on her life to serve. Her gentle spirit and humility shone from within and I didn't doubt the contribution she must have made to their church.

But I knew another wife married to a clergyman, a generation younger, who hadn't relinquished her career with joy. She yearned to make a difference according to her gifts and passions; to be seen as her own person and not just as "the vicar's wife." But sadly, she was thwarted in her quest at her church, partly because of warring factions in the congregation and partly because of her lack of an official role – and perhaps because of a lack of confidence. I wonder if her generation was caught in the middle of shifting perceptions. Many in the church still expected her to give up her work, so she acquiesced, but she saw other women blazing their own trails, following their callings, whether outside of the church or in. I wonder if she watched longingly. My heart went out to her while I prayed not to fall into the same trap.

Today people hold all sorts of expectations, including none, about spouses of clergy. If the man is the ordained one, his wife can play a more traditional role if she feels called to – or not. And the advent of ordination for women has resulted in a previously unthinkable person – the male clergy spouse. Though men married to ministers won't have the traditional roles expected of them, they face their own challenges. Namely, what is their role? Are they ignored during the coffee hour because they are married to the vicar? Are they expected to bake cakes and serve teas while bringing up the children, as has traditionally been the role of the vicar's wife?

The first time I appeared in public with Nicholas wearing a dog collar I oozed a self-conscious vibe. We were driving back from Guildford Cathedral after his ordination, stopping at the motorway services[2] to use the loo and get a drink. Walking in together, I was highly aware of the people around us and what they must be thinking, "Oh, one of those crazy Christians!"

This self-consciousness – the walking alongside oneself – can paralyze us. And ascribing attitudes or thoughts to others just isn't helpful; that day at the motorway services, probably no one even noticed the man and his dog collar or the woman walking next to him. Yet these assumptions can hold us hostage and become engrained. We begin to see life through a label; one that fits us ill but may start to define us.

I've sought to throw such a designation to one side and instead to live out of the gifts and calling that God has given me. For instance, at church I feel most fulfilled when I'm helping people deepen their faith in God. I love prayer; I love seeing how God answers the cries of his people. I'm not good with the making of many cups of coffee, not only because I don't drink the stuff but because I'd rather be out chatting with newcomers and regulars – especially as I seek to make connections between them and others in the congregation. A friend of mine calls this mixing and mingling my "vicar's wife duty." I don't mind the phrase as it's something that has grown out of my passions, but subsequent spouses of clergy might feel more comfortable behind the teapot or playing footie with the kids.

Taking on church roles out of sheer duty can mean depriving someone else of fulfilling their calling to serve. Of course there's a balance here, and we pitch in at times when we don't feel called but the need is great. And sometimes God beckons us into areas we might previously have eschewed.

A conversation with Michele Guinness, the wonderful author, speaker – and vicar's wife – helped me think through women's roles. She says that usually we can succeed at two out of three areas in life: family, work, and church. Her observation came at a crucial time as I wondered how I could manage all three as I tried to juggle time with the kids and hubs, my editorial and writing projects, and ministry at church. Quite simply, I couldn't. Focusing on two out of three – family and work – has freed me up and lessened the guilt over not being a superwoman who not only brings home the bacon and fries it up in a pan, but serves it to the wandering stranger.

But unlike my friend who doesn't bake cakes, baking I can do. My brownies, for instance, are the stuff of legend when it comes to church teas. One day a friend was serving coffee in the church kitchen as I presented my offering of oozing baked chocolate. "Oh, you'll have to give me the recipe for your brownies," she said.

"My recipe! Umm, didn't I mention that they come from a mix?"

Her face fell.

I said, "Sorry! It's the American way, I suppose; we go for ease and convenience. But these aren't any old brownies; they're Ghirardelli chocolate from San Francisco."[3]

Perhaps churches in rural communities hold more traditional expectations of their clergy wives than in cities. Our
London church boasts a cosmopolitan congregation, with
nineteen nationalities among the 150 members, and one benefit of the richness of this diversity is a lack of expectations
over the role of the clergy's spouse. Added to that, the majority
of our congregation are new to church, so they tend not to
have expectations of me rooted in history or culture anyway.

In short, I'm grateful that Nicholas doesn't pressure me to
arrange the flowers or make the tea or run the toddler group.
I think the best advice related to the role of the clergy spouse
is what I received when I was newly married and Nicholas
was still at theological college: "Be yourself." I would also add,
"Be your spouse's best cheerleader/advocate." And that's what
I endeavour to do.

When a publishing colleague heard I was marrying Nicholas,
he said from his previous experience as a pastor, "You'll always
have community around you." His comment brought clarity
to me as I approached the quick succession of churches that
Nicholas had roles with in the first half-dozen years of his
ordained life (two curacies and then his first vicarship). My
friend's advice echoed the words from the book of Ruth that
reverberated through me as we drove to Surrey for his first curacy: "Where you go I will go, and where you stay I will stay.
Your people will be my people and your God my God" (Ruth
1:16). These were now my people – warts and all. And I was
their people too – warts and all.

In each of the churches where my husband has served,
I've asked God for some friends. And in each case, my prayer
has been answered. In Surrey, my closest friends were of

non- English nationalities: Scottish, South African, and Irish. In northwest London, Nicholas and I enjoyed friendships with the two clergy couples and another couple in the church who then moved to Moldova for missions. Here in north London I revel in a wealth of friends, especially with my female peers. These I see as the true riches that God bestows on his people. In my years as a vicar's wife, I've witnessed many blessings and benefits of community. Alongside the many rich relationships formed in the good times, often a clergyperson and spouse will be invited into the depth of people's lives in times of crisis. Dear friendships have emerged through the stuff of tragedy; whether infertility, betrayal, death, disappointment, disease, or other. When we're asked to share in these moments, seeking God together, labels seem to disappear without a trace. The privilege of walking alongside someone in these seasons is one I don't take for granted.

Unfortunately, I've seen episodes of a community's down-sides too: backbiting, gossip, slander . . . It hasn't been pretty at times and it can be excruciating to watch from the side-lines, feeling that all I can do is pray. And yet the work of prayer can be the biggest struggle and task, for as Alfred, Lord Tennyson, said, "More things are wrought by prayer than the world dreams of."

I became a VW and a mother within six weeks of each other.[4] We moved into our first vicarage in September, Joshua was born in October, and Nicholas was inducted as vicar in November. So many changes came in a compressed amount of time that my head was spinning.

We made mistakes those first months; partly due to expec-tations, spoken or unspoken. How can newly arriving clergy (and family, if relevant) know what awaits them when they land in a church? How can a church know what the person in leadership – and their family – hopes for?

When Nicholas interviewed for the position, so many things about the church felt right: size, churchmanship, geographical location. But several things made us stop and consider, namely that the church secretary worked out of the vicarage's fifth bedroom, that the Sunday-morning crèche[5] met weekly in the living room, and that the photocopier was housed in the entrance hall. In short, the vicarage was overrun.

When the appointment panel unanimously offered the position to Nicholas, he accepted on the condition that we could reclaim the vicarage. "We do not want the secretary in the bedroom!" he said firmly at the interview, to raised eyebrows. He went about installing a separate phone line so that we could have a family line where I could make and receive calls without feeling like I was the unpaid secretary – this was before the ubiquity of mobile phones. He had two doorbells installed, again to separate out church and family life. We even went so far as to close the gate to the vicarage, though it turned out this was a mistake, for no one had told us that several kindly drivers parked in the drive[6] on Sundays to help their passengers who couldn't walk long distances.

We hurt some feelings as we established boundaries, but we were clashing with the practices instituted by clergy families before us. We also had to discern what the unspoken traditions were, and how they had emerged. As a fellow clergy spouse said, "You can put the fences up high and then welcome the people in."

Speaking of welcoming people in, let's visit the vicarage. I learned when I moved here that because the Church of

England is the established state church, and because it's been around in various forms since Augustine of Canterbury came to these shores in the late sixth century, it holds many historic assets. Churches dot the country, with every village boasting one. These churches need clergy, so vicarages were built to house them. Then church attendance fell and vicarages were sold and some clergy – mainly in rural areas – had to take charge of numerous churches, dashing on a Sunday from one service to another to another.

But the C of E still gives accommodation to its clergy and their families, and some, like us, get to live in one of the remaining original vicarages. Ours is a late Victorian, built in the 1880s, with lovely high ceilings, large hallways, and fireplaces in the majority of the rooms. Living in it is a privilege – it's huge, especially for London. I have my own study, Nicholas has his, the kids each have a bedroom and we have a guestroom. It's amazing, but like many vicarages it's draughty and mouldy and hard to heat. Funds are tight the nation over, so getting some released to fix the gate or mend the windows or add more insulation in the loft can be a struggle – though the London diocese treats us well.

Vicarage life can bring unexpected surprises, such as when people from the church walk into the family's living area, invited or not. They may have inherited the belief that they own the vicarage – like they think they may own the vicar. I've heard stories of vicarage dwellers being caught clad in pyjamas or in a state of undress when the vicar ushers in the churchwardens. Or articles that should be kept private somehow end up on display, like the time Nicholas hosted a school governor's committee meeting in our dining room. I had emptied the room of the clean laundry that had been hanging up and piled there, but the next day I had a shock when I saw one of my bras dangling from the radiator.

Other surprises can await us at the vicarage door. For instance, one night after Nicholas had left for his meeting, I took the usual evening precautions when answering the door: locking the inner door and securing the security chain. When I opened the door to the chair of governors, he seemed surprised at the chain blocking his way but soon realized he had the venue wrong. I hastily undid the chain and explained that we sometimes have casual callers seeking food and money, and that once one became violent.

At the end of the day, when I consider my role as a VW, what I hope I will fulfil is to love. After all, love binds people together and soothes disappointed expectations. Love sees people for who they really are, not someone foisted into a role or "just" a person in the pew. Love never gives up on hope, nor puffs itself up nor seeks its own agenda. Rather love bears all things, believes all things, hopes all things, endures all things.[7]

For as with so much in life, coping with a tag such as VW comes down to one's attitude and will. I can either inwardly bristle each time someone employs the term, or I can decide not to let it trouble me. Hopefully when Christ shines through me, the title will become redundant.

*7*

# WAITING FOR THE COMING KING

Several years ago, one Saturday morning during Advent, Joshua and I got up early to appear on the Saturday morning breakfast show on a Christian radio station. The forecast was for one of those rare dumpings of snow later in the day, which added to our nerves and excitement. As we got off the Tube and walked to the radio station, we glimpsed an explosion of pink and red in the sky: "Red sky in the morning, shepherds' warning."[1] Beautiful, but would we make it home?

I was on the show to give tips on making Advent more meaningful and Christmas less stressful. I spoke of the juggling act many people engage in at this time of year, what with nativity plays, Christingle and carol services, shopping, cooking, and how we can't do it all. We talked about how we can create time to seek God, asking him how he wants to use us to bring his light and life during the season. Maybe we could plan in advance, thinking through what we can give up from our normal schedule. Can we tolerate a house that isn't perfectly clean or clothes that aren't ironed?

I relayed a comment from a friend that sums up the foundational truth of the season well: "The thing that keeps my stress levels down most is to keep remembering that no matter what we do – or don't do – Christ still comes. Emmanuel is still with us. Even if we did NOTHING, Christmas would still be Christmas."

The live programme seemed to go well, and Joshua drummed up the courage to make a contribution. As we walked back to the Tube station, the snow started to fall. We made it home to bake another batch of cookies and watch the snow fall throughout the day. It fell, and fell, and fell some more. I started to wonder if we would rival the levels of snow in Minnesota, knowing that the snow-removal services would not be similar here. London and the Southeast would be paralyzed for days.

In the early afternoon we welcomed one of our amazing former au pairs who was visiting from Germany. While she partook in some Christmas cookies, sharing stories of her life and adventures, we enjoyed the cosy scene of the festive Christmas tree while looking out at the fresh covering of fluffy snow. We also made time to engage with the Posada that wends its way around the homes of church members during Advent.

Our associate vicar, a creative and caring woman who has lived in our community for many years, but who also spent a couple of years in Peru, introduced the Posada to our church. It's an ancient Mexican tradition, named with the Spanish word for inn, where in the weeks leading up to Christmas two young people dress as Mary and Joseph and travel from house to house, asking for a room for the night as they announce the imminent arrival of Jesus. The custom has changed over the years, and nowadays includes figures of the holy family and other characters travelling around and posing the question of how we will make room for Jesus.

That snowy day the children played with the pieces of the Posada and we lit a candle to remind ourselves that Jesus is the light of the world. We each tried to imagine how it would feel if we were one of the characters in the story, asking ourselves why we felt that way and what we thought God was doing. The kids drew and wrote in the Posada book, a special place to add prayers, photographs, and stories for the rest of the church community to see. Just as we finished, the doorbell rang, and we welcomed a mother and daughter who had traipsed through the snow to pick up the Posada. They, like Mary and Joseph, had made quite a journey.

For those who follow a church calendar, the start of the church year begins with the season of Advent. Traditionally those four Sundays before Christmas have been a period of fasting during which we prepare ourselves for the birth of Jesus. Some Christians are returning to this lost practice, making sure they have done all of their Christmas shopping, for instance, before Advent starts. They take the time and energy to prepare for Advent so that they can be ready for Christmas.

I laud them. I would love to be like them. But I haven't ever managed a complete fast from decorations or baking or even Christmas carols during Advent, for the cultural trappings of the season speak deeply to me of the spiritual meaning of Christmas. Growing up, I'd help decorate the Christmas tree much earlier than what Nicholas experienced – his family would purchase theirs on Christmas Eve, whereas my parents use the late November days just before or after Thanksgiving to put up theirs. As a child, I never knew of

Christmas carols banned during Advent, for I understood that the practical preparation of this season was part of the spiritual looking ahead.

When to put up the Christmas tree has been a source of conflict between me and Nicholas. His family custom coincides nicely with his theological one – that Advent should be a sober time of preparation, and that getting a tree on Christmas Eve is the best practice. Mine does not. Theologically I understand how erecting the tree later adds to the specialness of the twelve days of Christmas, but I love putting it up much earlier.

One reason is practical, namely that the process takes so very long, partly because I have views about lights. *Strong views.* I don't like blinking lights; I don't like gaudy lights. I don't like the British lights we have whose strands form a circle and therefore get kinked into knots. One year I was consumed with trying to untangle the many strands. Nicholas didn't seem to notice my labours, but after several frustrating hours, he walked by and said, "Why don't you take off the plug?"

"The plug?" I said, not understanding.

"Yes, you can unscrew the plug from the wires."

I had no idea, for American plugs don't screw off and don't have fuses in them. After taking off the plug, I untangled the wires in moments.

Stringing the lights on the tree is a labour of love, for I use loads for a full visual effect, making sure to wind them in and out of the boughs. When I've battled long enough, often getting scratched in the process, it's time for the fun of adding the Christmas ornaments. I've been collecting them for decades, a tradition that Nicholas welcomed. I think, *"Ah, the ornament we got at the Flagler Museum in Florida . . . and here's one we bought in Prague. Oh, there's the handmade nativity ornament Mavis brought back from Peru. And I love this cute little reindeer that Margo gave me at college . . ."*

I would love to spend Advent in quiet reflection, praying and preparing for Jesus to be born in my heart and home, but instead I mix the reflective with the practical as I get ready for the feasts of Christmas. Because the British traditions differ from the American, over the years I've worked hard to ensure that Christmas feels like Christmas in this foreign land. What could feel like a situation of scarcity – the pain of being away from loved ones during the holidays – has evolved into a season of abundance as our traditions have developed and solidified. Finding myself in Britain means creatively enacting the American approach to Advent and Christmas, while learning the British one too. And more importantly, making sure the Christian elements, which transcend any culture, receive the star treatment.

A prime way I make Christmas feel familiar in the foreign-land-that-is-home is to bake Christmas cookies, for they are part of the American psyche. They feature at Christmas parties and coffee mornings; they form the perfect accompaniment to a friend dropping over; they make a tasty and satisfying dessert. And because cookies are still somewhat of an oddity over here at Christmas, I bake and bake and bake some more. They become our gifts to the church team, friends, and staff at our kids' school, and through their hand-crafted drops of sugar, butter, and flour, they speak of love and tradition and celebration.

The Advent wreath and Advent calendars play another important role in our family's observing of this season of waiting for Christmas. At the centre of our kitchen table we place a candelabra that we decorate with greenery. The candles are three purple and a pink with a white one in the middle. People name the candles differently, but we tend to follow the tradition of the first purple candle signifying Abraham and the patriarchs, the second Moses and the prophets, the third candle the rose one for Mary, and the fourth purple one for John the Baptist. Candles are lit adding one per week, until finally on Christmas Eve or Christmas Day we light the white one in the middle, signifying Jesus. Our kids adore eating dinner by candlelight, for we cover the table with tea lights and festive candles to add to the spectacle, with fairy lights sparkling in the window.

Advent calendars have morphed in the culture to now being mainly chocolate countdown calendars. Many Christians rue the change, but part of me appreciates the honesty. If Christmas now means only a family day of feasting and a present exchange, then why keep up a charade?

But for many Christian families, the Advent calendar is a meaningful way to build up the anticipation to Christmas. Our favourite one is the three-dimensional scene with little characters who get added each day, starting with the star on top of the manger, then the angels, then sheep and cows and wise men and shepherds and camels and finally the holy family. Joshua, being older, figured out that with twenty-four characters to reveal, and with the Baby Jesus always being last, that he should be ever so kind and let Jessica go first. She soon twigged, and now they alternate turns.

One Advent practice that I love, but that I hadn't encountered before coming to the UK, is the Christingle. I know many churches use this delightful symbol on Christmas Eve, but in our church we hold a special late-afternoon Christingle service at the beginning of Advent. The custom came about in Germany in 1747 when a minister wanted to explain the gift of Jesus and used items from creation to do so. Modern-day Christingles follow in the tradition he started: an orange symbolizes the world; in the centre a lit candle stands for the light of Christ; a red ribbon around the orange represents the blood of Christ. Four sets of cloves, or skewers with raisins stuck on them, symbolize the four seasons and the bounty of the earth.

Many churches follow in the prayer that the German minister prayed for the children: "Lord Jesus, kindle a flame in these dear children's hearts, that theirs like thine become." In our church, the service is a favourite one, with the children excitedly holding their Christingles in wonder in the darkened church, with their parents furtively glancing from child to child, hoping they won't set light to the hair of the woman in front of them. At the end of the service we enjoy fireworks in the vicarage garden and a boisterous tea in the church centre.

Another favourite service that takes place in Advent, though strictly speaking from the view of fasting it probably shouldn't, is the carol service. Our church becomes transformed by the addition of beams hung above the chairs, on which sit rows of candles and greenery. The trick is to avoid the seats directly under the candles, for even though each one nestles on a foil tray, somehow the dripping wax finds its way onto one's favourite red sweater and is a pain to remove.

The congregation and wider members of the community enjoy the lessons and carols – the readings from Scripture telling the overarching story of salvation – interspersed with songs of praise. And afterwards, mince pies and mulled wine. Okay, I can understand the appeal of gently heated red wine on a chilly night, spiced with cinnamon and flavoured with orange. But mince pies? A waste of calories in my book.

I have a pile of Advent devotionals that I've acquired over the years, and every year I assemble them, wondering which one I should read. I start with a day or two of readings, but more years than not, my attention scatters. (And yes, I see the irony in admitting this, as writing devotions is one of my favourite things.) With a jolt I then remember the "Christ in Christmas" bookmark stuck in its hiding place in my bookshelf; I grab it with a smile and dive in. It's based on a NavPress book and traces the Christmas story with plenty of Old Testament prophecies as well as the New Testament story of the birth of the Messiah.

Last year while following the process I outline above – choose a devotional or two before remembering the book-mark – a new spiritual practice emerged. It wasn't something I planned or anticipated, but seemed to find me on that first Sunday as I started writing a poem based on the reading from Isaiah 9:2–6. I penned a poem each day, some better than others. The practice of chewing over the words of Scripture, and expressing them again in my own words, makes the truths sink more deeply from my head to my heart.

One important figure in the lead-up to Christmas culturally is Santa Claus, as I knew him growing up, or Father Christmas, his moniker in the UK. Call us killjoys, but Nicholas and I de-cided not to foster a belief in Santa in Joshua and Jessica. As we thought about pushing on them a story of a benevolent person whom we say is real, whom they never see, and then who turns out to be just a myth, we became more and more uncomforta-ble. Would they then not trust us about the reality of Jesus, the source of benevolence and the giver of all good gifts?

Right or wrong, we've been upfront with our kids, telling them the truth that the modern-day Santa is based on a fourth-century bishop, Saint Nicholas, who gave gifts secretly, including putting coins in the shoes that were left out overnight. His saint's day is 6 December, which my parents would celebrate when I was growing up by filling our shoes with some candy and maybe a small gift.

Joshua, being a sensitive child with an often serious bent, hasn't minded knowing the truth behind the secret. But Jessica, brimming with imagination, sometimes longed to believe – for the fun of it. I don't know if we've chosen the right path with this decision; some Christians integrate Santa seamlessly into the celebration of Jesus' birth, without confusion or conflict.

Whatever our cultural background, and however we observe Advent, for those who follow Jesus, this season can be an important time to prepare ourselves for the coming Christ. We anticipate; we wait; we welcome the second coming of our Saviour. We long for the fulfilment of his promises, for the time when he returns and every knee will bow and every tongue confess that Jesus Christ is Lord.

8

# THE LIGHT OF CHRIST HAS COME INTO OUR WORLD

As the Advent wreath glows brightly, candles burning, the cookies are baked, empty boxes of decorations are stored back in the loft,[1] presents are wrapped and stashed under the tree, and the reality of Christmas happening dawns on me. The excitement of Joshua and Jessica kicks into high gear as the countdown reaches its culmination. Jesus Christ is born into our lives.

Our first Christmas as a married couple, when Nicholas was a curate, I tried to replicate exactly what was happening with my family back in Minnesota. I had never missed a Christmas with them as each year I'd fly back from Washington, DC, where I lived, to the family home. But having married a minister, for whom Christmas was a working holiday, the expectation of a guaranteed snowy holiday evaporated.

My mother's German roots inform our gatherings at Christmas, and like many Northern European families, our main celebration of the holiday would occur on Christmas

Eve. Around four or five pm, we'd go to church, always delayed when we were children by my usually on-the-ball mother who would forget something and need to go back inside (so that she could play Santa, putting out the gifts). After church we'd either dive into the presents or enjoy our dinner: the former when we were very little; the latter when we were old enough to wait and knew who Santa really was.

That meal I tried to recreate our first year was the traditional (to me) homemade chicken noodle soup. Before moving here, I would tell people about our feasting on this unusual meal on Christmas Eve because of the German roots. Then I moved to the UK and we welcomed a succession of German au pairs into our home. One after the other looked at me blankly when I told them about our chicken noodle soup tradition, saying that not only did they not eat such a meal at Christmas, but they hadn't even heard of such a practice. I felt deflated. Then, five au pairs in, finally one of them nodded in agreement. Turns out her mother's family was Russian originally before settling in Germany. Because of the Russian connection, they'd partake of chicken noodle soup on special days, including Christmas Eve. I felt vindicated, and wondered if my German relatives had Russian roots.

That first Christmas Eve, Nicholas and I were on our own. I had never before made the egg noodles for the soup, although I had watched my mother plenty of times. Knowing that Nicholas avoids white bread, I decided to use wholewheat flour instead of white. I also liked, when eating my mom's soup, the bits of noodles that were slightly thick and chewy, so in this first attempt I didn't roll out the batter very thinly. I made loads of noodles, thinking that if I was going to invest the time in such an exercise, that we should benefit from having enough soup to freeze to enjoy later. I boiled up a chicken and hoped for the best.

The soup was a disaster. The stock was more like hot water, without much flavour, as I had used only one chicken and had to keep adding more and more water to the broth as the noodles absorbed the liquid faster than I thought possible. The noodles turned out to be a clumpy mess of stodge, especially because of the wholewheat flour. After taking a spoonful I burst into tears. Phyllis Boucher I was not.[2] The frustration over my failed cooking attempt highlighted my deeper pain at not being with my parents, siblings, and adorable five-year-old niece and three-year-old nephew. What had I done in coming to this country?

We called my American family to wish them a merry Christmas, and it wasn't long before my tears took over and I squeaked out how sad I was to be in England and not in Minnesota with them. My dad, wise and gentle, said, "Amy, you longed to be married. Now you are, and your home is with Nicholas." He gently but firmly helped me to follow the biblical injunction to leave and cleave.

That disastrous first batch of soup, and the poignancy of trying to create everything just like it was in Minnesota, changed the way we approached Christmas Eve in the years that followed. We kept the importance of Christmas Eve from my point of view, but widened the celebrations to include people from the congregation, which makes the evening richer and more celebratory. Each year we host a big Christmas Eve dinner, inviting some people we know well, some we're just getting to know, and some who might not receive many other invitations during the holiday season.

Our kids can't imagine Christmas Eve any other way, with the feast sandwiched between the crib service, which is friendly to families, and the midnight service. With a nod to my heritage of opening up all of the presents on Christmas Eve growing up, the kids open their stocking gifts when they get home from the crib service. They also get to do so without restraint, not having to wait their turn between presents, a system we enforce later.

Our meal starts with a smoked-salmon starter,[3] something Nicholas particularly likes, and then we move to the centrepiece of the homemade chicken noodle soup, which I've now perfected. Although one year, I faced a chicken noodle soup crisis again. I had boiled chicken after chicken, removing the meat from the bones and condensing down the stock into something delicious. I used about five chickens for a huge batch, and about eighteen eggs for my noodles. When I assembled my soup on the day before Christmas Eve, my professional-sized stockpot was full, so I put the remaining soup into another pan. It was cool outside, but not freezing. After I set the soup outside in the garage overnight, I decided that I hadn't added enough carrots. So I chopped and boiled some up, adding them to the big stockpot outside. I went to bed, content with my efforts.

On Christmas Eve we attended the crib service as usual, enjoying the full church of regular attendees and visitors. I skipped the refreshments afterwards so that I could attend to the last-minute preparations for our feast together. I arrived home, went out to the garage, and retrieved the soup. Opened the lid and caught a whiff of something foul. In vain I tried boiling the soup up to rid it of its smell. I nearly cried as I threw that huge stockpot of poisoned soup away. Thankfully the other small pot was fine, and somehow we had enough to serve our guests. When I recounted my sorry tale to my parents later, my dad said, "You had the perfect conditions to grow bacteria – just like a petri dish."

Along with the usually good soup, I add a special green salad, which my British friends aren't sure about eating in the winter, topped with the moreish caramelized almonds and dressed with raspberry vinaigrette. And homemade breads, usually pumpkin raisin for one and blueberry orange for the other. For dessert we feast on Christmas cookies and ice cream – the culmination of all of those weeks of baking. Our British guests aren't sure what they're getting into with this quirky Christmas Eve dinner, but many seem to enjoy it after they realize that the soup tastes better than they may have feared.

In between the courses we read the Christmas story and share in some prayers, thinking about how Mary said yes in obedience, Joseph believed the angel, God revealed his plan to lowly shepherds, and Jesus who is God is born in a stable. The mixture of prayers and Bible readings with laughter and tasty food never disappoints.

The evening ends with the late service. I wish I could attend, but thoughts of a random fire in the vicarage with our precious Pyelets there compels me to stay at home. Instead, I enjoy the Christmas tree, looking at the lights, trying to ignore that pesky strand that went out, and call my family in America. With the time difference, they are in the midst of their Christmas Eve festivities, opening presents or cleaning up after dinner. We talk and I imagine the scene, faces a year older, living room uncharacteristically untidy with wrapping paper and boxes strewn around, a plate of cookies on the dining-room table, my brother talking excitedly about his gifts.

Incorporating the key parts of my childhood Christmases into our Christmas Eve celebration has brought richness and meaning, I hope not only to me but to my family and our guests. But then the next day is Christmas Day. And while I would love just to eat leftovers from the night before, Nicholas needs a roast turkey dinner for it to feel like Christmas.

Christmas morning dawns, the morning after the night before. Nicholas is shattered from the intense run-up to Christmas and the late night, having washed dishes after getting home from the service. There's another service in the morning, so no rest for the weary. The kids know that opening presents in our home is stretched out so they don't have a big incentive to get up early, although they open one present before church. Normally breakfast is nothing too special as we drag our tired bodies out of bed, but one year an au pair made a gorgeous stollen to start off our day – nothing like a shot of sugar to get the heart racing.

Families don't crowd to our Christmas morning service, so Joshua and Jessica delight in being selected to add the baby Jesus to the nativity set or to light one of the candles on the Advent wreath. We belt out our hymns in praise to the God who came to live in and dwell among us, joyful for Immanuel.

And then home to Christmas lunch. Having lived here for so long, I now understand the importance of this meal: the turkey, the stuffing, the sausages rolled in bacon, the roast potatoes and gravy, the bread sauce, the vegetables – especially the Brussels sprouts. Christmas pudding for dessert – or Christmas cookies, for those who prefer. Sort of like the energy that goes into making a Thanksgiving meal.

I'm afraid I don't go for homemade when it comes to Christmas lunch; I know that sounds a sacrilege. It's all I can do to make another big meal after the performance from the night before. So we have roast potatoes out of a bag from the freezer section; a turkey-breast roll thingy again from that same section in the supermarket. Veg and at least lovely homemade gravy. Nicholas graciously doesn't complain; after all, he's not able to cook the meal because of spending the morning at church.

We sit in the dining room, usually the four of us, the delicate German wood pyramid we bought in Heidelberg spinning under the heat of its candles in the centre of the table. We cross arms and pop the Christmas crackers, but I draw the line at donning the paper crown. We stop and share the moment, enjoying each other and the knowledge that the season of baking (for me) and service preparation (for Nicholas) has ended, and now we and the Pyelets can enjoy together the twelve days of celebrating Christmas. I often want to shout, "Christian, reclaim the twelve days of Christmas and the spiritual discipline of celebration! Don't take your tree down on Boxing Day!" Indeed, many Christians like to leave their tree up until Candlemas (2 February), enjoying the lights in the darkness of winter in the northern hemisphere.

Sometimes I wonder if the miracle of Jesus dwelling among us is as much of a joy for clergy as is the relief of getting to the end of an intense period of planning and executing extra services, gatherings, school visits, and other festive activities. As we dine on our Christmas meal, Nicholas starts to relax a bit. We make sure we finish in time for that hallowed British tradition, the Queen's (now of course the King's) Speech, at three o'clock. Through watching each year my ambivalence about being the monarch's subject dissipated as I witnessed the late Queen's commitment, sacrifice, and service to others. As the longest reigning monarch, she seemed to become increasingly bold in sharing her faith in Jesus Christ during her annual speech in the latter years of her life.

And then it's time for opening presents – one of my favourite activities. The kids have waited all day and the moment finally comes to root around under the tree and distribute the packages, making grand piles of presents at each person's feet. The needles of the tree start to fall off at an alarming rate as the presents jostle the branches, and I worry about my favourite crystal ornaments that sway from side to side.

Cultures and strong views can clash during our time of opening presents. Nicholas's family puts more emphasis on exchanging cards than presents, so gifts have not been part of his heritage. He doesn't enjoy spending money, and finds the excess of consumerism a challenge, thinking of the many children around the world who won't receive any gifts. My family, on the other hand, expresses love through gifts; my mom and sister are experts not only at spotting great deals but at finding just the right gift for their recipients. Different backgrounds plus different approaches to spending money plus different expectations to giving and receiving gifts plus a whole lot of tiredness can equal conflict and disappointment.

And so we have learned to manage the opening of gifts. We enjoy a chunk of them after the Queen's Speech, and then leave the next batch for the next day. And sometimes the day or two after. Although for me the immediate impact is lessened in terms of the sheer emotional spectacle of opening all the gifts at once, I acknowledge the benefit of stringing out the pleasure. Our kids learn the joys of delayed gratification, and also to value the gifts that they open instead of descending into a crazed maniacal rush of opening gift after gift without really looking at any of them.

One year when Nicholas was a curate, we cheekily invited ourselves over to the home of close friends for Christmas lunch. I found it fascinating to watch my friend prepare the meal that means so much to those in Britain. She had a particularly challenging time that year, as her oven chose to go on the blink that very morning. She had to use a neighbour's oven and it all seemed a hassle, but she managed to pull off a tasty meal with panache. I was intrigued to see her warming the plates with boiling water, for Yanks don't tend to take these measures even when we have a working oven.

We enjoyed our feast with them and their young daughter, and later were even more glad to have been a bit forward in joining them for lunch, because after several years the husband, one of Nicholas's best friends, died of cancer. We had the gift in the memory bank of regular days spent with them, walking in the New Forest as he and Nicholas talked history or music, as well as that special holiday.

For that's the thing about holidays, we don't know when the next one will be the last "normal" one. Change can come in a moment, such as through accidents or betrayal. Or maybe we are already living a new normal, facing the loss of a child, spouse, parent, or friend through accident, disease, or betrayal.

The sense of heartbreak and anguish came back to me the Christmas of 2014 as I witnessed scene after scene in public and closer to home: A bin lorry[4] in Glasgow careered out of control in the city centre, killing six people. A terrorist siege in the Lindt chocolate café in Australia brought fear, with two dying and three injured. A public figure in her thirties died of colon cancer on Christmas morning, ten minutes before her 5-year-old twins woke up to ask if it was time to open the stockings. Another mother of small children, this one dear to one of our Christmas Eve guests, collapsed of a weak heart and died on Christmas Eve, leaving her husband and two young daughters. Our friend felt the urge to contact his best man on Christmas Day and heard the shocking news. These tragedies have made me think a lot about the word *heartsick*. For my heart feels sick at the thought of the families grieving during Christmas as they miss their mothers and sisters and fathers and sons. Over those with debilitating sickness who can't join in with the opening of presents or feasting around a table. Over the senseless violence that brings about death and weeping. Truly, our hearts feel sick.

Life changes every day, and because we inhabit a fallen world, that change can be unwelcome. But our culture views holidays such as Christmas with a standard of perfection – we need a day with no conflict but happy families, with no one missing from the table. We feel disappointed when we can't achieve that state of joy and contentment.

I suppose this longing for completeness hearkens back to the true meaning of Christmas. That cute little baby born in dire circumstances was both man and God. He came to live on earth and then to dwell in and among his people. During Advent we're waiting for the coming of Jesus, not only to celebrate his coming to earth as a baby, but as we yearn for his coming again. That second coming when he will wipe all the tears from our face; when he'll make the conflicts cease; when he'll heal the broken hearts and release us from our crushing disappointments. We'll be completely well; fully human; totally overcome with joy and reality and the fullness of life. With the aged apostle John on the island of Patmos, we say, "Come, Lord Jesus."

And although we long for his second coming, we celebrate his coming to earth at Christmas, ushering in his kingdom of light and love. True, in his second coming all tears shall cease, but God also wants to set into place his kingdom in the here and now. As his redeemed people, we are given the mind-blowing task of collaborating with God to bring his kingdom of light, life, peace, and love here on earth. Jesus is born in our midst, and we welcome him. We ask him to invade our cells, bringing healing; to shape our emotions, that we may show love; to impart peace as the Prince of Peace; to show us how to party as the giver of new wine.

Sometimes we experience grace upon grace as his kingdom invades our lives. A friend of mine, Geraldine Buckley, who is British and now American, having lived much of her life in the States, shared online the gift of God breaking in one Christmas:

> This has been a dream of a Christmas. It started with the night of December 23rd, when two lovely young women, missionaries far from home, asked if they could come round as they were longing to wrap Christmas presents. They were the sweetest, most charming 19-year-olds and I made them thick hot chocolate served with pumpkin bread straight from the oven, and we giggled together, and they wrapped. All my presents. Beautifully. Magic! Bless them, bless them.
>
> Then there were delightful Christmas Eve services with friends, and then with family – both churches alive with love, and excitement generated by the age-old glorious story and impending festivities. Our family's traditional reading of Christmas classics around a roaring fire under the gentle light of a huge, beautifully decorated tree, all the family gathered this year.

Christmas Day with carols, and roast beef, and laughter, and movies, and Christmas pudding. And peace, and grace, and lots of love. Boxing Day lunch with more family festivities – and then tonight a party in a friend's gorgeous Victorian house. She gathers people who love words and music, supplies desserts so scrumptious that angels would add an extra halleluiah to their singing should they sample them – and then people share stories, and readings – and tonight besides words there was a harpist, and sixteenth-century Spanish Christmas music, and soft light that washed over vibrant paintings and entranced faces . . . It was good – it was all so good.

In the great lottery of life there are Christmases – and then there are Christmases. There are the Christmases of childhood filled with wonder. But then there are others filled with heartache, disappointment, hurt, loss. Some are spent away from home and are lonely, lack-lustre; some are just fine. Just.

Like many of us, I've had my share of all of those times. But occasionally you get one that is full of love, and healed relationships, and peace, and sudden unexpected glimpses of God, and what the true meaning of the feast is all about. Moments of heart-lifting, breathtaking joy pervading the security of grace-filled familiar traditions – and that's when magic happens. Christmas magic. This was one of those Christmases. Thank you, Lord.[5]

May we know the love of the Christ child who makes all things new and imparts his creativity, joy, and peace to us. To us a child is born. To us a son is given. And he shall be called Wonderful Counsellor. Mighty God. Everlasting Father. The Prince of Peace. The one who makes all things new – even the new year.

# 9

# THE NEW YEAR DAWNS

A once-in-a-lifetime happening, the turning of the new millennium. A relative newcomer to these shores, I watched with interest the plans for marking the occasion. The Millennium Dome would be, we were promised breathlessly, the ultimate experience, whether we visited on New Year's Eve or during the year 2000. Workers cleaned up the toxic waste from a derelict site near Greenwich for the creation of this new London landmark. Although Tony Blair, then Prime Minister, hailed it at its opening on New Year's Eve as "a beacon to the world," its twelve zones were roundly mocked as being lightweight – especially the Faith Zone. The Dome morphed into a white elephant, sucking a million pounds a month in operating costs before it closed due to the small number of visitors. In the years following, it saw a few temporary gigs before it reopened in 2007 as the O2, named for the communications company who gutted and redesigned it. They launched the massive entertainment complex with a concert by Bon Jovi, and finally the Dome was a success.

The Millennium Wheel, as it was then named, fared better. Instead of closing after a year, as intended, it was rebranded as the London Eye and now is the most popular paid attraction in the UK. I've been on it more than once, and can attest that Nicholas excels as an unofficial tourist guide. Not only does he point out the obvious attractions along the winding Thames, such as Big Ben and the Houses of Parliament, but he names places further afield, such as Crystal Palace, Battersea Power Station, and Lord's Cricket Ground. His historical commentaries are the stuff of legend – when he was in his twenties and went on a group tour of London, his new friend soon abandoned the official guide to listen in on Nicholas's insights.

And what about Y2K? Can you think back that far? It was before the days of social media, but I recall the hype and fear-mongering, especially in America, forecasting that we'd experience massive electronic failures when computers changed from 1999 to 2000. Some hunkered down with generators and stockpiles of food and water, waiting for some kind of apocalypse. Michael Hyatt, the social media and leadership guru, wrote *The Millennium Bug*, which reached the *New York Times* bestseller list. Now its marketing description induces cringes: "At the stroke of midnight on January 1, 2000, the world could erupt into complete chaos. Imagine: social security checks stop coming, planes all over the world are grounded, VISA balances skyrocket, and the military, police officers, and firefighters walk off the job."

The British response, in contrast, was wonderfully calm and understated.

The move from 1999 to 2000 felt momentous, but why, I wonder, does our culture hype up the turn to a new year?

Aren't we just marking getting older? (Of course, that is something to celebrate.) I suppose it's an excuse to party – people expect that we'll imbibe loads of alcohol as we lose our inhibitions and dance the night away.

But a deeper reason may lie in the promise of a new start. We yearn to leave the old behind and enjoy a clean slate; maybe, we think, this will be the year for the fulfilment of that long-held dream. Maybe we'll lose that weight, get fit, stop drinking/smoking/gossiping, stop fighting with our spouse and kids, find a spouse and have kids, write that book, get that promotion, win that award, get out of debt, love that neighbour, and so on, and so on, and so on. New year equals new start. As Christians, we can incorporate a time of giving thanks for the year that's passed while looking ahead, with God, to the coming year – thereby including some prayerful reflection with our bubbly.

I've appreciated learning about the Scottish approach to the New Year, which they've emphasized because in the sixteenth and seventeenth centuries, the Church of Scotland frowned upon the celebration of Christmas – Christ's mass – as too Catholic or as rooted in a pagan midwinter festival. They didn't see a biblical basis for the holiday, holding this stance for about four hundred years. Celebrating Christmas was even banned by law from 1640 to 1686.

The tradition of a quiet celebration of Christmas persisted until well into the twentieth century, with it only becoming a public holiday in 1958, and Boxing Day not until 1974. So it's not surprising that the Scottish celebrate the new year instead, with New Year's Eve known as Hogmanay, a word that could have Scandinavian, Anglo-Saxon, or French roots.

Several Scottish friends shared some of their customs and the accompanying roots, such as the influence of Celtic Christianity and its pagan foundations: "The house is cleaned, sweeping in the direction of *out* so all the bad stuff is symbolically got rid of." As they cleanse and prepare for the new, they rid themselves of the old as they empty bins of rubbish[1] and wash their clothes, hair, and bodies.

The first-foot tradition might leave you scratching your head if you're unfamiliar with it, as was I. People interpret it differently, but the practice is to ensure good luck for the house by having a tall, dark-haired male cross the threshold first in the new year – a throwback to the Viking days when a blond stranger meant danger. The first-footer comes bearing gifts laden with symbolism: a piece of coal to represent the provision of warmth through the year, and shortbread or the New Year special cake – a rich fruitcake with hardly any flour in wrapped in pastry – as a symbol of provision of food. As one Scottish friend remarked, "We children would 'first-foot' all our friends as a sign of maintaining our friendships in the new year." Another, who lives in Hampshire, keeps up the tradition, saying they "ask the friend with the darkest hair visiting us on 'Ne'er Day' to bring the coal, shortbread and whisky. It really bemuses our English friends, who think it all very odd!"

She also weighs the practices carefully with her Christian faith: "There are lots of traditions and customs, some of which are verging on superstitions, so I don't adhere to all of them in our home. But it's nice to open the windows to let the new year in, be first-footed with coal, whisky and shortbread and eat steak pie."[2]

I like the idea of cleaning out the old and preparing for the new, with the physical act of cleaning the house symbolizing the cleansing we ask God to do in our hearts and souls, washing away that which is sinful and ushering in holiness and purity. We can also amend the practice of opening the windows to ask God's holy wind to sweep into our lives, bringing the breath of life and renewal.

I think I might adopt some of these practices for our family. After all, Nicholas has a Scottish great-grandfather . . .

A more universal practice at the start of a new year is to decide on some New Year's resolutions. I'd venture we've all made them, and later let them go. Instead of resolutions that I'll soon abandon, I try to adopt spiritual practices, following the wisdom of such writers as Dallas Willard and Richard Foster. For instance, one way I ring in the new year is to reflect back on the previous twelve months by reading through my spiritual journals – reviewing the year before the Lord. I know not everyone likes keeping a journal, but for me they are a lifeline and a prime way I engage with God. As often as I can, I commit to a practice of reading the Bible and praying. I write out my prayers, allowing myself to be brutally honest, acknowledging that God knows my heart anyway, and try to quiet myself to hear the Lord's still, small voice.

Rereading my journals, and noting the highlights and lowlights, brings back the year just gone. I remember incidents I had forgotten and often uncover jewels that get buried in the rush of everyday life. The cries of my heart on one day may look self-indulgent in the light of the events that transpired on a later day. And when I take the time to reread my highlights from years gone past, I see the Lord working, not only with prayers fulfilled, but in those deep cries that he didn't answer in the way I longed for.

I love reading through my journals because they instantly transport me back to the sights and smells of the moment. The journals bring alive, say, our five-week summertime trip to the States, including an epic road trip where I introduced my island-dwelling family to the wonders of the great land mass that is America, with its wide highways, rolling farmlands, and down-home cooking and hospitality. As I read, I relive the enriching conversations with friends and family from whom we are usually separated, and I picture the succession of beds we slept in.

We're all made differently, and for some, writing is an arduous experience, something that doesn't bring life and meaning. But if you're one for whom it feeds your heart and mind, I can't recommend the practice of spiritual journaling enough – including looking back over your words at least once a year. Out of my prayer times are ideas birthed, dreams documented, damning words of irritation or frustration or self-centredness confessed, forgiveness received, and hope imparted.[3]

If you're not the writerly type, have you considered other ways to look back as you move forward? Perhaps you could flip through your diary,[4] glancing through your engagements and asking God to shed light on the various activities and experiences during the months. Or you could go through your photos from the previous year, again to refresh your memories of God's goodness. Or if you're a social media dweller, scroll down your posted content and conversations to see what was worthy of your online thoughts.

May we learn to pause and wonder, reflecting on God's goodness and mercies, which are new every morning.

When I heard buzz over a new book, *My One Word*,[5] I got myself a copy, in late January nonetheless, and delved into it. It's a simple exercise that produces profound results. Before God, choose one word for the year. The word will be something we can remember and return to throughout the weeks and months; it will best reflect what we hope God will do in and through us. The word can inspire and encourage us; it will motivate and challenge us. According to the authors, the ten most-chosen words are trust, patience, love, discipline, focus, faith, surrender, peace, listen, and joy.

I loved the idea, and have incorporated it as a spiritual practice for the last decade. Some of the words that I've felt reverberate as those for the year have included *flourish*, *train*, and *breathe*, with accompanying verses. For *train*, for instance, I thought the implied meaning would be training for righteousness – the work of sacrifice and graft; saying no, no, no; focusing down. Coming from my hard-working parents, who both grew up on farms in the Midwest and whose grandparents were immigrants, I naturally gravitated to this interpretation. But several people reminded me of a different way of looking at the word, one based in horticulture. As writer Tanya Marlow remarked, "You train a vine to grow in a certain direction, pinning it where it doesn't naturally go, so that it begins to grow in a different direction."[6]

Looking back, I can see how her interpretation is more apt than my original one. Throughout the year, God moulded my character as I submitted to his plans for my wellbeing – which didn't end up being the ones I thought were best. I said yes to obedience and pruning, which felt painful and constricting but brought about growth. By being intentional about choosing one word for the year, I could give thanks even during the painful times, understanding that God can use trials and disappointment for the training and growth of my character.

Might you consider choosing a word for this year, whatever month you're reading this? It may sound an overly simple exercise, but I've found it a clarifying, enriching experience. If not a word, perhaps a prayer or verse from Scripture for the year. Resolutions may be easily broken, but the spiritual practices we undertake will bear fruit that lasts.

As for New Year's celebrations, I may not swing from the chandeliers or be the last one to leave the party, but through adopting an intentional attitude over giving thanks for the old and welcoming the new, the turn of the calendar now drips with meaning.

# 10

# COME TO MY PARTY!

January strikes dread in the hearts of many; in the UK it's a cold, damp month following the excess and parties of December. The monotony of the short days, with darkness closing in during the early afternoon, can bring downcast spirits. In recent years, the idea of Blue Monday has popped up, propagated first by a travel company and then by a drinks company. They claimed the third, and then the first, Mondays in January as the most depressing day of the year. After all, weeks have passed since Christmas, the debts are coming due, people feel guilty about not keeping resolutions, and overall, life is tough. That a travel company championed this new concept first – so that we'll book a holiday to raise our spirits – and a drinks company next – that we'll dive into alcoholic spirits to raise our spirits – makes me stop and consider. I wonder if these companies think they can manipulate us into buying their goods and services through creating a new social phenomenon.

To me, January isn't a downer but a special month. When I was a girl, the early weeks were filled with anticipation for my birthday towards the end of the month. Then the big day would arrive, complete with presents in the morning with the family, and later cake and a party with my friends. What could be better in the heart of winter, especially in the frigid Minnesota cold that makes playing outside for more than twenty minutes a dangerous activity?

January in Washington, DC as a twenty-something didn't seem too bad either. We might have experienced a big snow-fall during the month, but I liked that, as it made me think of Minnesota. The month was sure to have a birthday gathering of some kind, for my friends were fantastically social creatures.

No, I didn't mind Januarys.

And then I married Nicholas, and January held another reason to be special. We began planning our wedding during my September trip to the UK when we were newly engaged. (Two surprise engagement parties! A surprise punting trip down the River Cam! Life in this picturesque country was so romantic! Exclamation mark, exclamation mark.) Nicholas was in his final year at theological college, and so after looking at the term times, we thought the options for a wedding and international move looked tricky – either December, after Christmas, which seemed much too quick being three months hence, or June, when the summer term finished, which seemed a terrible wait for two lovestruck people desperate to live in the same country. We met up with the wise and caring principal of Ridley Hall, Graham Cray, and presented him with our dilemma: December or June? December or June? We're ever so consumed with December or June. As our conduit of God's wisdom, he showed us a third way.

"Why not," he said gently, "think about January? Nicholas, you could start the term and then miss two weeks to get married, enjoy your honeymoon, and move Amy over here. It would be good for her to experience life in Cambridge in the community before you begin a curacy."

Thus our wedding at the Falls Church Anglican (one of the first Anglican churches in Virginia; George Washington was a vestryman[1]) took place in January. So now with an anniversary and birthday to celebrate that month, I don't think of Blue Mondays or failed resolutions. I think of new beginnings and God's surprises that shatter my preconceived notions about how life will be.

A few years ago, I decided to cast aside any acquired British reserve and throw myself a birthday party. My ulterior motive was to build friendships and foster community among some women whom I didn't know very well from church and the kids' school. I got the idea from the lovely Michele Guinness[2] who hosted such a party to befriend some interesting women in their then new church. I had resisted throwing a party for some time, wondering if my friends would think that I was angling for a bunch of presents, or that I wanted selfishly to celebrate the great and wonderful *me*. But the thought lodged itself within me, so finally I decided to give it a try one January. As I was discussing the party with a friend, she suggested that everyone take turns answering a thought-provoking question during the meal. What a wonderful idea, I mused, to give shape to the evening and to help everyone feel included. And then people wouldn't feel like they only talked to those on their left or their right. I trawled the Internet for questions that could be answered at a deep or a more surface level, depending on how much one wanted to reveal.

Nicholas and I have since adopted this practice of asking open-ended questions at some of the dinner parties we throw. Here are some more general ones:

- What would be a special treat for you?
- What's a favourite childhood memory?
- Who would you invite to your dream dinner party?
- What is your most treasured possession?
- What keeps you awake at night?
- Where would you like to live?
- If you could bring something extinct back to life, what would you choose?

And some more probing ones:

- Who has had the greatest influence in your life? Why?
- If you could write your obituary, what would you say?
- Who is the kindest person you've met? Why? How did they impact your life?
- What's a goal that you'd like to accomplish in your lifetime, and why?
- If your house was burning down, and your family was safely out, what three objects would you rescue and why?
- If you had a time machine that could take you to one point in history or the future (and back), which point would you choose?
- If you could wish for one thing to come true this year, what would it be? Why?

During the evening, Nicholas agreed to be the waiter but left us on our own between courses, working on his sermon in the kitchen. Several of the women said I shouldn't be cooking on my birthday, so offered to bring a dish. That lightened the load. For fun, I put together little party bags for my friends of some scrummy chocolate truffles that I also included in the dessert course.

God answered my prayers for the evening. I had asked him for the right mix of women, that the open-ended questions would lead to enriching conversation, and that people would get to know each other better. I even experienced a moment of transcendent joy as my friends sang happy birthday to me. As I took in their shining faces, I felt them bestow on me a gift of unalloyed joy; an outpouring of love. I'll raise my glass to that!

Speaking of parties, think not of gatherings of like-minded friends, but of the dread of parents as they prepare to host a kids' party. With our big vicarage and money-scrimping ways, we've only hired out other venues for our kids' parties twice, favouring the at-home approach for the other ten experiences. We soon learned about managing the size, however, for when Joshua turned 4, we made the mistake of inviting seventeen kids, thinking that a good percentage wouldn't come. We were wrong, and had even a few more kids when some younger siblings tagged along. What a big sigh of relief we breathed when we waved the last child away, parents having retrieved them.

When Joshua turned 6, he was in the throes of his obsession-with-royalty phase, especially Queen Victoria. We decided, with his consent, that instead of his guests giving him presents, they could donate anonymously to either of two funds if they wanted – one to give Bibles to children in

Tanzania and another to a Joshua-to-visit-Balmoral kitty. We were heartened by the generous response of his friends, and were thrilled when the Bible Society's newsletter ran the story, along with a photograph of some children in Tanzania receiving Bibles from the money raised.

For the multitude of parties we've held at home, we've worked out a timetable with military precision. One favourite time-tested game, however, was new to me: pass the parcel. Never before had I heard of this game, loved by children the country over, but I soon learned its necessity. A friend told me that she learned the hard way that her austere childhood means of playing it wasn't acceptable to her son or his friends; it wasn't good enough to have one treat at the very end, but each layer needed to reveal a mini-treat.[3]

Whether for adults or children, parties are an opportunity to practise the spiritual discipline of celebration. When I was in my twenties I learned about this concept, advocated by Dallas Willard, and made all the more special as I enjoyed the rich celebrations of my small team of work colleagues who were like an extended family. They knew how to celebrate, whether for birthdays or Advent teas or graduations, complete with beautiful decorations, sumptuous food, rich conversation, and deep laughter.

Many Christians overlook this spiritual practice, sadly sometimes because of restrictive teachings at church. Perhaps we've never thought of celebration as something we can do unto God, or the cares of the world seem too strong, or we exhibit a spirit of scarcity rather than the abundance God would have us embrace. We only need to look to the Bible as a model – check out Jesus' first miracle of turning the water into wine at the wedding feast in Cana, for example (John 2). The Old Testament bursts with stories of celebration, such as that in 2 Samuel 6 of King David leaping and dancing before the Lord with all of his might. He rejoiced at the gifts of the Lord and wanted to return thanks, doing so with abandon. But not everyone approves of all-out celebration, such as Saul's daughter Michal, who saw David and despised him in her heart, saying to him, "How the king of Israel has distinguished himself today, going around half-naked in full view of the slave girls of his servants as any vulgar fellow would!" (v. 20). But he stood firm, replying, "I will celebrate before the LORD. I will become even more undignified than this" (vv. 21–22).

As we see with King David, celebration is rooted in gratitude to God for the many gifts he gives us. I love how Dallas Willard puts it in his classic *The Spirit of the Disciplines*: "Holy delight and joy is the great antidote to despair and is a wellspring of genuine gratitude – the kind that starts at our toes and blasts off from our loins and diaphragm through the top of our head, flinging our arms and our eyes and our voice upward toward our good God."[4]

Might you throw a party for yourself this year, whether in January or June?

# PART 3
# MARCHING INTO SPRING

# BY THEIR ACCENT SHALL YE KNOW THEM

On one of my yearly trips back to the States to visit family and friends, the kids and I made a pilgrimage to our favourite chic-but-cheap retailer, Target. When there I stock up on things I can't get in Britain or buy items that are less expensive, to haul back to the UK. We were standing at the checkout line,[1] placing the items on the conveyer belt as we waited for our turn. When I took out a Dr Seuss-related item, in a package of six, Jessica exclaimed, "You're buying rubbers!"

The man ahead of us in line flinched but I said, "Yes, they're for your birthday party." I added quickly, "But in America, we call these *erasers*."

She remained blissfully unaware of what must have been going through the mind of the man in front.[2] Differences in language can make for some interesting exchanges.

Before I married Nicholas, my boss, Os Guinness, an Englishman-in-America, warned me that the little differences between the two countries would jar me at first. He was right, and nowhere as much as with language.

I knew that the British and Americans employed different terms, especially for things like cars: to me bonnets were quaint headpieces adorning Jane Austen's characters; a boot was just that, something to wear on your foot, especially when living in the West; and in my first year in the UK when I tried to explain that a woman's muffler was hanging off her Range Rover, I stuttered and stammered, searching for the correct word. Finally I pointed to the back of her car and she said, "Ah, the exhaust!"

So although I knew I'd struggle with dustcarts and, back then, the name for a pay phone (call box? pay box?), trousers versus pants, chips and crisps and biscuits and crackers, what I didn't understand was the *hidden* meaning of language. Namely what Brits really mean behind their polite words or ironic remarks.

Perhaps you saw a graph that was making the rounds on social media, reportedly developed by a Dutch company trying to do business in the UK, which aimed to decipher some of the cryptic meanings of British sayings.[3] One column states what the British say; the next defines what the British mean; the third reveals what foreigners understand. So "I hear what you say," means, "I disagree and do not want to discuss it further," but is taken as, "He accepts my point of view." Or, "I only have a few minor comments," means, "Please rewrite completely," and is understood as, "He has found a few typos." No wonder we foreigners get our knickers in a twist.[4]

I didn't have the luxury of such a graph when I first moved here, so learned by making mistakes. My husband and I soon differentiated between a British *nice* and an American one – how nice was that person or meal or gift really? But it took a bolshie[5] literary agent, when I was a commissioning editor at one of the big publishing conglomerates, for me to learn that the British and Americans mean different things with the word *quite*. When I said that I thought her client's proposal was "quite good," she didn't withhold her disgust at my assessment of her project – I thought I conveyed its merit, but she heard me say that the proposal was lacking.

This literary agent eschewed cultural convention in educating me about the difference in the meaning of the word, as I learned from a fascinating account of the English by an English anthropologist: *Watching the English*.[6] Kate Fox speaks of how the English don't often say what they mean, and attributes this reserve not so much to historical reasons but because of an innate social awkwardness. The English, she says, can talk about the weather if provoked, or if you're walking a dog in the park you can connect over canine matters. But to say what you really mean instead of mastering irony and understatement can be awkward or scary or intimidating.

Added to the meaning of words is the thorny issue of accents. I was happy to lose some of my nasal Midwestern inflection and word choices when I moved to Washington, DC, when in my twenties (substituting soda for pop, for instance), but a decade later when I moved to the UK, I didn't fancy changing how I spoke. And yet I was painfully self-conscious about opening my mouth; any foray into a shop would label me as other – as foreign – as soon as I uttered a word. So I would keep schtum[7] as long as I could, and would wait for the look of pity or surprise when I asked for my change or said thank you.

Early on, at a lunch given by one of Nicholas's fellow theological students, our host held up a jar of spices and asked me to say the name of it. I naively answered, "Oregano," (oh-REG-ah-no) to which the party erupted in laughter. My host explained that the British would say, "Or-rey-GAH-no." I smiled with them, masking the sting of their amusement over what was normal to me.

Some Americans who have lived in the UK for a long time acquire a mid-Atlantic accent; some aspire to it, seeing it as a step up in terms of class. (Received Pronunciation, of course.[8]) Others simply can't help it, for their use of language unconsciously moulds itself to the person they are speaking with, as Jo Saxton, a Brit-in-the-States friend, encountered when checking in to a flight. She was amused to see the pained look on the check-in clerk's face as she realized that she'd accidently imitated my friend's accent throughout their conversation – a bad Dick Van Dyke rendition – including saying "Cheers" as she bade her farewell.

Jessica has this same ability to pick up accents; when she's in the States, her pronunciation morphs into a true middle-Atlantic sound. The Yank in her starts to exert itself and the way she says *water*, for instance, loses any distinctive strong *t*. I love the transformation, but the change doesn't last long; after a few weeks back in the playground the accent fades away. Not completely though; sharp-eared observers can hear a slight inflection – so much so that the head teacher[9] commented after her performance in the nativity play, "We've never before had an American Mary!"

This small island hosts a mind-boggling number of accents. England alone boasts the peculiarities of the Geordies or the West Country or Manchester or Birmingham or the vastly different accents, according to them, of those from Yorkshire and Lancashire. I haven't forgotten Liverpool, whose accent travelled across the Pond with the city's most famous sons. And we haven't even mentioned London, with the tones of the East End versus North London versus South and everything in between, including the multi-layered accents informed by the Caribbean. Nor, of course, the huge number of non-native English speakers living in the UK, whose inflections bring new lyricism to conversation.

Before moving to the UK, I was one of those Americans who never differentiated between accents in the English language. Indeed, in my twenties I worked in Virginia for an Englishman, as mentioned above, and took for granted that his Received Pronunciation (RP) was standard. In my work I came across people from around the world, including a visiting Australian, whom I mistakenly thought was English.

Received Pronunciation, I've learned in my years here, is rooted in the public school[10] system. For in the past, at least, public schools considered themselves to have failed if, when the pupils/students left, their regional accents were still intact. Indeed, Nicholas acquired his received pronunciation this way – through the good but sometimes painful experience called the King's School, Canterbury. This way of speaking also became known as BBC English, because only the products of public schools were seen to be intelligent enough to read the news. I've been fascinated to witness the shift away from Received Pronunciation at the BBC as they moved one of the London studios to Manchester and now showcase different accents to shed any lingering label of elitism.

For accents denote not only regional differences around the United Kingdom, but that all-pervasive issue of class. Open your mouth, some say, and I'll tell you where you sit on the social ladder. From the cut-glass vowels of the upper class to the dropped consonants further on down, accents reflect issues of social standing.

In those first months in the UK, when we were living in Cambridge and Nicholas was finishing off the last term of theological college, some of the spouses went to see a just-released movie, *The Full Monty*. Afterwards I compared notes with another American, also newly married and newly transplanted. We understood the gist of the story – stripping isn't hard to get – but much of the dialogue left us stumped.

We weren't the only Americans scratching our heads. As I was writing this chapter, I smiled at the following update on a social media site: "From Worldcrunch: 'It took a London court a full hour before realizing that a woman who was testifying was in fact not speaking English but Krio, a distinctive Creole from Sierra Leone.' This may shed light on why I need subtitles when I watch British TV."

Another American filled in the missing pieces for me: "Krio is an English-based 'pidgin' language that originated out of the Gullah dialect of the American south. I understand it better than many regional British dialects!" She continued, "Wonderfully pregnant language. And the speakers play with it as they go along. Instead of superlatives, they'll double the word. For example, Paul's statement, 'I have finished the race,' is translated, 'de race is done done!'"[11]

I love the idea of piling on the words for emphasis; reminds me of Hebrew, where the Lord is not only double holy (holy, holy), but the unthinkable, mind-blowing, triple holy (holy, holy, holy).

And my accent? It's no longer the predominately Scandinavian sounding tongue, with long o's and a nasal inflection. Some Americans might think I've gone to the dark side with the patterns of speech I've developed in order to be understood on this side of the Atlantic. Like my life, my accent is American with influences from my years in Britain – an online post from a friend that alerted people to a radio interview I took part in highlighted my "soothing, anglicized American voice". And my many years of living in the UK, especially my years in multicultural London, have mainly cured me of a self-conscious standing outside of myself when it comes to my patterns of speech. In London, I'm one of many accents, and frankly, as a Yank, not terribly interesting at that. Although when I'm hosting a group of visiting Americans I feel branded a tourist, especially on the Tube as I gauge the sometimes withering glances of those peering over their newspapers at us.

Often when I'm outside of London, the reality of being an American in Britain comes back to me in a rush. I spent some time writing in Eastbourne a few years ago, revelling in the quiet of a friend's house and generally speaking to no one except during my daily phone calls to my family. The sole person I talked to was in the local store and, sure enough, he asked me where I was from and how long I was visiting. Or when I stayed with a friend in Carlisle and we ordered pizza, the delivery person quizzed me about my accent. In some parts, I guess, I'm still an anomaly.

I still struggle to understand accents outside of RP, especially those of various parts of the North. When recently we visited Newcastle, I was fascinated to hear so many people speaking just like Cheryl Tweedy.[12] Why I was intrigued reveals more about me, of course, than the accent. But no wonder she didn't make it on the US X-Factor – Yanks couldn't comprehend what she was saying.

Some British people think that I and other Americans living in their country should adopt their pronunciations, arguing that American English and British English are actually two different languages. A transplanted American, therefore, should speak the language of the United Kingdom, such as if they moved to, say, the Philippines and learned Tagalog to be able to communicate with their new neighbours. I can't go with this argument though, for to me, adopting the British accent feels like I'm taking on airs and pretensions – saying things in a perceived posh way that isn't true to who I am.

I have adapted the way I talk – employing British words where the American one isn't understood or appropriate (trousers instead of pants; pavement instead of sidewalk, jug instead of pitcher, and so on). When I go back to the States or talk with Americans, these words fall away, although sometimes I get stuck and can't remember the American word. I'm also informed by family members and friends that my inflection has changed, following a more British pattern.

Although I've mostly lost that self-conscious standing-beside-myself feeling, sometimes someone will notice my accent and ask me where I'm from. "North London," I'll respond with a bit of cheek, knowing that's not what they mean. Then I'll add, "But from the States originally." And again I'll be jolted into an awareness of otherness; that sense of being a foreigner in a strange land. And again bubbling up will be the longing for home, which God embeds into each of us, whether we live in an adopted country or not.

For one day, we will dwell with him in that new home, with people of every nation, tribe, language, and tongue, and no one will judge us on the way we speak. There will be no more class or distinction or division, for the Lord will heal the confusion of the languages that he introduced at the Tower of Babel, when the people outstepped their boundaries.[13] What a glorious day that will be!

Until then, I see language and accents as a source of richness. When meeting someone new, for example, I can now discern a bit about them by the way they speak and use it as a point of introduction as I ask them about their heritage or country of origin. Accents can become a door to understanding the life and times of another, which is something to celebrate, for I love learning about people's experiences of home and their journeys in life, whether they've moved country or stayed in the same region or town.

# 12

# "BEHOLD YOUR KING!"

Now is the healing time decreed
For sins of heart and word and deed,
When we in humble fear record
The wrong that we have done the Lord.

*(Latin, before twelfth century)*

When I moved to the United Kingdom as a resident alien, I had a month before Lent started – some time to adjust before I would engage in the season of examining myself before God, seeking his grace, forgiveness, and renewal. Or so I thought. I didn't enjoy that honeymoon period people talk about when one embraces a new culture – when everything is bright and shiny and fascinating. When we landed at Heathrow, I was woozy from the speed of the wedding, the Australian flu I had endured during our honeymoon, the whirlwind of packing up my life's belongings into boxes and suitcases, and the pain of saying goodbye to my loved ones. I had so focused on what I was leaving that I didn't much consider what I was coming to.

As we drove the bigger-than-we-originally-ordered hire car,[1] stuffed to the brim with suitcases and bags, to Cambridge, I sat numb in the passenger seat, which was situated on the opposite side than what I was used to. I knew that British cars were different to American ones, with a right-hand drive, but now these cars would be the norm of my life, and not a curiosity. What would my new life involve? I simply didn't know.

As I observed quirks and differences between the cultures as we drove north and east, Nicholas's mind was elsewhere. He was considering the assignments he needed to complete and the activities of college life he would re-enter – and introduce me to. To him this was home, and the fluke of his semester abroad and subsequent trips to see me in Virginia and Minnesota were behind him.

We made it to our flat in the student accommodation, and after surveying the small quarters that would be our first married home, I unpacked. Eager to connect with my family and friends back in the States, I assembled the components of my desktop computer. This, by the way, was long before smartphones and tablets – we still connected to the Internet by a wire plugged into the wall. I had a shock, literal and figurative, when I pressed the power button, for with a poof and a flash, my computer died. Through my tears I realized I should have switched the voltage from 110 to 220 on the back of the machine. I was stunned at the financial implications, but I was more grieved to think I couldn't now connect with my family and friends in the States.

And so began my life in the UK. I felt thrilled to be united with my husband, the answer to years of prayers, but I felt the pain and loss of leaving all that I knew and held dear. And that moment when my computer died I sensed that my journey would often entail these two contrasting emotions – joy and sorrow – at the same time.

I was crippled by my life changes in those first few months. I missed my family and friends and wondered what my role was, especially as I wasn't allowed to work, for Nicholas's sending diocese covered the cost of our rent in Cambridge as long as I wasn't earning income. I knew I should use the six months as a gift, to get to know my new country – and husband – and adjust. But with Nicholas at lectures, I would mooch in the flat and flip between the channels, all five of them, settling on movies from the fifties. When he'd come home and ask me about my day, I'd say with a tear or two, "All I did was watch classic movies. It doesn't matter how I spend my time."

Yet I had moments of light and life as I settled into Cambridge, enjoying the picturesque setting as the snowdrops, and then daffodils and tulips, burst through the muddy ground. Walking by the River Cam, browsing at the market, waking up next to my husband, sitting in on a theology lecture by the renowned theologian Jeremy Begbie – at times I had to pinch myself that this really was my life. But then the rush of emotion would come back to me as I realized how far I was from my family and friends, and I'd have to work hard to be grateful for the good things before me.

So Lent mostly passed me by that first year, with me too overwhelmed to set my attention to spiritual practices. The next Lent came around, when we were situated in our home in Surrey during Nicholas's first curacy. I had found some freelance editorial work and loved my upstairs study with its bookcases and hilltop views, so I thought I was strong enough to fast or add a special devotional reading. I soon abandoned the practice in a heap of emotions, however, saying to a visiting American, "All of life is Lent." I felt I had relinquished so much that I couldn't face giving up more.

Through the years of Nicholas and I creating our life together, a blend of the Old World and the New, I no longer think of life as an unrelenting Lent. After all, we all face times of Lent in the form of challenges and losses, whether the death of a loved one, a debilitating disease, the dream that never materializes, the betrayal of a friend. What I've come to know in a deeper way through my separations is that God through his indwelling Holy Spirit accompanies us on that journey of smiles and tears. He never leaves us when we feel lonely or sad; when we miss a loved one or rue a poor decision. When all of life feels like Lent, he holds our hands to let us know he is with us. And he helps us turn our aches and longings into the solid hope of heaven, giving us an eternal perspective.

The day before the start of Lent, Shrove Tuesday, seems to have more of a cultural impact in these shores than in the land of my birth. Even those who wouldn't dream of giving up something for Lent will enjoy their meal of pancakes (crepe-like ones, not the big American blodges of carbs) on its eve. Savoury to start and then the classic lemon and sugar to finish, or chocolate if you're feeling decadent.

I still associate pancakes with breakfast, even if I only rarely eat them now. Once in my work as an editor I met an author – a visiting American – for breakfast before a conference and we went to a local café. As one who doesn't love an English fry-up, the menu left me searching. But under the dessert menu I spotted that they made pancakes, so I inquired if I could have that for breakfast. The waiter squinted at me with incredulity, but he served me in the end. At least I knew not to ask for maple syrup.

After Shrove Tuesday comes Ash Wednesday, a day when Christians often fast from food as they mark the start of Lent. This act of devotion I followed when I was single, but it was the first spiritual practice I threw out the window when I coped with the changes in culture. And after we had children, I gave up attending the Ash Wednesday evening service as well. I miss receiving the ashes on my forehead and hearing the words that remind me of our mortality: "Remember that you are dust, and to dust you shall return. Turn away from sin and be faithful to Christ." Caring for the kids rather than going to the service, though, means I can read and pray in solitude.

More years than not I turn to my favourite book written for the Lenten period, *Reliving the Passion*, by Walter Wangerin.[2] A master storyteller, the author writes as a participant – sometimes a close bystander, sometimes a character – of the narrative of Jesus' last days. He transports us to a vivid world of sights and smells that bring alive the Easter story, thereby engaging not only our heads but our hearts.

When I read his book, I'm there at Bethany, seeing the woman pour out her extravagant love for Jesus. I feel Peter's desolation after his betrayal of Jesus. I sense the blackness and despair of Good Friday. I rejoice at the wonder of the resurrection, the empty tomb. A good book can not only inform but spark one's imagination, as this one has done for me over many periods of Lent. I echo Thomas Jefferson: "I cannot live without books."

As the strangeness of living in a different country began to wear off, I slowly adopted some of the spiritual practices of my previous life, including a Lenten fast of sorts. God revealed to me riches in my lonely times, as he heaped love on me and helped me to look outside of my situation to that of others.

And I found out to my delight that Lent is made of forty days – which I knew previously – but that the time between Ash Wednesday and Easter Sunday is actually forty-six days. Sundays are feast days – times to celebrate the resurrection of our Saviour, and thus no fasting is required. I immediately adopted this view, wondering why I had never heard about such a fantastic practice, rich in meaning.

Part of Lent is Mothering Sunday, a new phenomenon for me. (And note that the official name is Mothering Sunday, not Mother's Day.) Always the fourth Sunday in Lent, it's not the day in May I would associate with mothers. I enjoyed learning about the history behind the holiday – that it was created so that those working away from home could have a Sunday off to visit their mother church – and their mothers. The workers, often agricultural or domestic servants, would walk home, picking flowers on the way for their mums.

In contrast, the American holiday of Mother's Day always falls on the second Sunday in May. It was first celebrated in 1908, in honour of the founder's mother. She, however, became disillusioned when in the 1920s the holiday became over-commercialized.

The year I was pregnant with our first child, I didn't think that we would celebrate Mothering Sunday for me. But when we met my husband's family at a restaurant, I was surprised to see, not only at my mother-in-law's place setting but at mine also, a mug saying, "For a special mum." I took the mug with mixed feelings, first, not resonating with being a *mum*, for my title of love for my mother is *mom*, and that's what I aspired to be, and second, because I knew I had a long road ahead of mothering before I should warrant such a moniker – being only pregnant didn't seem enough. But I received the mug as a gift of promise for things to come.

With Mothering Sunday being a busy church day for Nicholas, and to honour my American roots, we celebrate Mother's Day in May, and not on Mothering Sunday. I enjoy receiving a bunch of daffodils on Mothering Sunday, along with the other women in church, but look forward to a more relaxed celebration in May. A tricky holiday, with many people dreading it if they were never able to be a mother, or if they had or have a difficult relationship with their mother, or if their mother has died. May the Lord make us sensitive and caring.

For me, Holy Week brings with it a mixture of welcome and unease. Welcome, as we ponder the mind-boggling sacrifice of the God-man who died to set us free. Unease because of how exhausted Nicholas will become as he plans and takes so many services. The demands on church leaders are great, even though he has care of only one church, in contrast to rural vicars who dash between three or four, or more.

Then we reach Good Friday, which some might say is the holiest day of the year, when Jesus who is God died on the cross to remove from us the judgement of our sins. Our church holds a three-hour service of meditation, starting with hot cross buns in the church centre before launching into the half-hour meditations. I never fail to be moved by the power of the day.

One Good Friday I penned a poem lamenting my role in crucifying the King:

O Jesus of Nazareth,
Thorns we twisted and turned

Upon your head we placed,
Crowning you King of the Jews.

Upon you we spat;
With a reed we struck your head.
Kneeling in homage, we mocked,
With our lips; with our hearts.

Crucified, we crucified,
Nailing you to the tree
Watching you wither and bleed
As darkness came over the land.

From deep you cried out,
Not at us, but to your Father:
"My God, my God, my God –
Why have you forsaken me?"

Those words cut to our soul
Reverberating from within
We watched you breathe your last,
And the curtain was torn in two.

From what we have seen and heard,
Indeed, from what we have done,
We echo the words of the centurion,
That truly the Son of God you are!

Good Friday is all about the cross, but I wonder if we see the cross as something merely wooden. For instance, in a previous church I attended, one of the preachers, no matter what he was speaking about, wove into his sermon the cross of Christ. And yet in those sermons, I felt that he viewed the cross as static – something that signifies that Jesus died on the cross for our sins, and if we receive him into our hearts, we can have assurance of eternal life. I'm not denying that as truth; it forms a central meaning of the cross and its impact on our lives. But my understanding has been enriched by deepening that truth of the cross as a living place of exchange for the people of God.[3] So not only do we receive saving redemption from Jesus' sacrificial act, but we receive ongoing forgiveness and love and affirmation from the Father.

Here's a spiritual exercise I've found helpful to release the power of the cross. As we spend time quietly before God, perhaps holding a small wooden cross, we can confess the sins committed against us, picturing ourselves taking them to Jesus on the cross. What do we see the Lord do with the things we leave there? Do they disappear into him? Turn to ash, or into a shoot of young growth? A key is to be specific, such as naming such examples as that nasty exchange with our spouse this morning before breakfast; the feeling of pain we experience when that boy bullied us at school, bruising our arms with his pinches and hurting our hearts with the names he called us; the friend who snubbed us. The Lord gives us freedom from these hurts, showing us that he'll never turn his face from us.

And at the cross we can confess our sins. Perhaps it's pride – we think we don't need anyone else. Or envy, that insidious belittling of God's gifts in others. Or gluttony, when we don't exercise the Spirit-given gift of self-control. Or slander or gossip or malice or lust . . . The cross of Christ relieves us of any and all of our wrongdoing, when we confess it to God and receive his forgiveness. A key part of this exercise is not to miss out on receiving whatever God wants to give us as we come to him.

If we incorporate this spiritual practice into our lives, we find we have a means of embodying the hope of Easter as we shed our old selves and embrace the new. We know that God dwells in and through us by his Son and Spirit, enabling us to collaborate with him in ushering in his kingdom of life and peace.

After Good Friday, and Holy Saturday, we wake up on Resurrection Sunday, when all things are made new and joy pervades our beings.

## 13

# BEING EASTER PEOPLE

After the sombre examination of Lent comes Easter morning – Resurrection Sunday. And the first words Nicholas and I exchange, bursting with joy, are, "Christ is risen! He is risen indeed! Alleluia!" For the fasting ceases and we embrace the feast. The central story of our faith reaches its climax and we reverberate with the joy and wonder of Christ, our God who rose from the dead and lives again. The resurrection changes everything, bringing hope and new life – the kingdom of God here on earth.

My first Easter in the UK wasn't spent with outbursts of joyful acclamations. Nicholas and I went to the tiny rural church on the outskirts of Cambridge where he was experiencing ministry in the countryside, a place where a few weeks before I'd been informed by a crotchety old man that I was sitting in *his* pew. As was the tradition of my church in Northern Virginia, I dressed carefully for the Easter service, putting on my pink dress and pink shoes but deciding not to don my pink hat. I also grabbed my warm raincoat, knowing the church was chilly – and not only because of grumpy men with lord-of-the-manor tendencies.

I went, I worshipped, and I returned to our small flat, not having removing my coat once. Not only did I need it for protection against the cold, but I realized while looking at the casual outfits of those around me how much I would have stood out as an oddity. People didn't wear dresses in pastel hues for Easter in rural Cambridgeshire, and definitely sported no hats. I started to suspect that a Hollywood rendition of an English wedding, complete with Hugh Grant, did not relate to ordinary life in Britain.

I held back on my tears of homesickness during the service, but released them a couple of weeks later when an older woman from my church in Virginia sent me an order of service from Easter Sunday. Seeing the familiar typeface, I broke down, missing my friends and colleagues and all that felt like home from that friendly place. Memories came flooding back when I read the words for the opening hymn, "Jesus Christ Is Risen Today," as I heard in my mind's eye the strains of the organ and the thousand voices raised in worship. My experience of the chilly rural church, where I didn't talk to anyone and where just a few people murmured hymns that I didn't know, seemed a sad substitution for what I had left. I didn't realize then that I was accessing another layer of grief.

Over the years, however, shafts of sunlight broke through the clouds and "joy came in the morning." The culture shock wore off and I learned to fit in, not wearing dresses of questionable fashion but allowing myself to dress up more than others might as an act of celebration and respect. I entered wholeheartedly into the Easter celebrations of hope and new life as I stopped looking back, making the church where we worshipped "my" church – even through our quick succession of them.

We buy the kids a chocolate egg at Easter. These large eggs were a novelty to me when I first arrived, as Americans don't go for this ostentatious, oversized display of cultural Easter spirit. Instead, Americans fuel their kids before church through an Easter basket, which lands in the child's room (or which they have to hunt down), filled with peanut-butter eggs, puffy marshmallow chicks, jelly beans, small chocolate eggs, and other goodies. Sunday mornings in a vicarage home can be stressful, but somehow we all make it out of the door, eager to fuel life and excitement in that wonderful greeting at church, "Christ is risen! He is risen indeed! Alleluia!" We worship and sing and listen and enjoy the Lord's Supper together. And at our current church we benefit from a creative idea of our associate vicar. Several years ago she proposed we place a large children's-sized table at the front of the church. During the distribution of Holy Communion, the children are welcomed to the table, where they receive bread and grapes (unconsecrated) with the gentle command, "Remember that Jesus loves you." More often than not a holy silence descends as giggles and shuffles cease. A woman sitting next to me commented on how loud school dinners can be, and how quiet in comparison is the table at the front.

After church, home to a favourite Easter happening in our vicarage, although not as regular as I might wish – the Easter brunch. Brunches are becoming more common in the UK than they were when I first moved here, when the thought of combining breakfast and lunch into one meal eaten mid-morning was anathema. With our Easter service occurring bang during prime brunch time, I can't follow the custom properly, but we can invite people around after church to wonder at the strange American combinations of food. The thought of an egg-and-sausage casserole/bake accompanied by cinnamon rolls and fruit salad screams my mom's famous brunch. Her astounding cinnamon rolls are so good that my kids want to film and post online some videos of her teaching us how to bake them.

We build up to Easter with a forty-day season of reflection, and yet we seem not to celebrate more than a day. Tom Wright, the prolific and engaging theologian, rues this oversight. He says that Easter ought to be a long festival

> with champagne served after morning prayer or even before, with lots of Alleluias and extra hymns and spectacular anthems. Is it any wonder people find it hard to believe in the resurrection of Jesus if we don't throw our hats in the air? Is it any wonder we find it hard to *live* the resurrection if we don't do it exuberantly in our liturgies? Is it any wonder the world doesn't take much notice if Easter is celebrated as simply the one-day happy ending tacked on to forty days of fasting and gloom? It's long overdue that we took a hard look at how we keep Easter in church, at home, in our personal lives, right through the system. And if it means rethinking some cherished habits, well maybe it's time to wake up.[1]

I agree with him; as Christians we should be known for the joy that marks our faces and our characters as we exude hope and grace. As I've learned on my journey to finding myself in Britain, in this life we will face disappointment, disease, and hardship, but as God's beloved, his promises and gifts should change our disposition. He helps us to forgive; he gives us hope and strength; he showers us with grace. As St Augustine of Hippo reminds us: "We are an Easter people and our song is 'Alleluia!'"

I wonder if being an Easter people means that we retain a childlike sense of wonder and gratitude. When I think of these attributes, a friend pops into my mind, Mary Matheson, whom Nicholas and I refer to as our fairy godmother. She was in her seventies and a prayer partner of mine when I was single and pining for a husband. She spotted Nicholas on his own at our church one Sunday, invited him back to lunch at what she called her old people's home, and delighted in linking us together. She always expected God to surprise her and revelled in his answers to prayer, such as Nicholas and me coming together.

She exuded that childlike wonder in God, calling herself the Narnia kid and looking out for Narnia-like lampposts in her day-to-day life. She had weathered many storms – her husband divorced her when their six children were young, and she had to cling to God for provision and hope – but her faith and joy never left her. She loved being one of the young members of her retirement home, which she afforded through a generous grant – more evidence of the God who met her needs, not only emotionally but practically too. She died of cancer during Holy Week several years after I moved to the UK. I imagine she spent that first Easter in the company of Aslan, regaling the company of saints and angels with her stories and poetry.

Some of my friends take celebrating Easter more seriously than Christmas. This isn't popular in our culture, not least because of the contrast between the cute baby at Christmas and the bloody reality of the crucifixion, as one friend commented: "Many are happy to accept [Jesus] as a baby, but his teachings and adult life make them uncomfortable and demand something of them."[2] This reminds me of Jesus' parables; not everyone responds to his teachings. We might find that sad, but it's part of God's mind-boggling plan of letting us exercise our own wills and judgements.

The sheer amazement of Jesus' sacrifice grips many: "Easter is the fulfilling of God's plans. I am always awestruck at how much God loves us and how far he is willing to go to save us and bring us back into his family."[3] I love the visceral effect of another friend's thoughts that she shared in a discussion online:

Easter is more important than Christmas for me. A few years ago I was asked to speak to a small group at school about how important Easter was to me, but when I started talking about Jesus dying on the cross for me, I burst into tears, and was sent to the staff room to get a drink. I felt such a wally, but my bursting into tears actually spoke more to the children than any words I said.[4]

A God who was willing to take on bodily form, be born in humble circumstances, be tortured and wrongly accused and even die for us – it's stunning and amazing and awe-inspiring. As is how he rose into new life and now dwells amongst us through us living "in Christ," in the apostle Paul's words.[5] I'd love to shout it from the rooftops!

So if Easter is so important, how can we regain a hearty celebration of it? More advice from Tom Wright, from his inspiring book *Surprised by Hope*. He says if Lent is a time to give things up, then Easter should be a time to take things up, employing a wonderful garden image to contrast Lent and Easter:

> Of course you have to weed the garden from time to time; sometimes the ground-ivy may need serious digging before you can get it out. That's Lent for you. But you don't want just to get the garden back to being simply a neat bed of blank earth. Easter is a time to sow new seeds and to plant out a few cuttings.[6]

From my scant experience of gardening I know the pain and stiffness that the removal of weeds can leave on my body the next day. But if we do all the clearing-out work without planting something new, weeds will take over the empty soil in time. Yet when we plant vegetables or flowers or shrubs, we'll benefit with herbs for the kitchen, lavender for the bees, beautiful colours to assail our senses. Bishop Wright continues:

> The forty days of the Easter season, until the ascension, ought to be a time to balance out Lent by taking something up, some new task or venture, something wholesome and fruitful and outgoing and self-giving . . . If you really make a start on it, it might give you a sniff of new possibilities, new hopes, new ventures you never dreamed of. It might bring something of Easter into your innermost life. It might help you wake up in a whole new way. And that's what Easter is all about.[7]

If we embraced the season of Easter – the forty days after – as a time of new beginnings, what might be birthed in our lives? I think of new ministries for pregnant teens or serving the homeless at a soup kitchen. Or finding the courage to visit our neighbours; to stop and chat in the park; to make eye contact and smile at the young mum whom we met some time ago. Or a new creative venture such as a book of poetry, a painting, spending time prayerfully colouring in Celtic designs, setting up an online support network for other like-minded people. The answers are as individual as we are, but what joins us together is Christ dwelling in us, inspiring and transforming us.

Jesus didn't leave his disciples during the forty days after he died, but appeared to them many times. Reassuring them that his life and death and miracles weren't just a dream or a figment of their imagination, he promised to pass his power and love along to them so that they could preach, teach, and heal in his name. Then after forty days, Jesus ascended to heaven and ten days later the Holy Spirit descended into God's people at Pentecost. Now we never are alone.

But think back to the pre-Pentecost days, the time in between the resurrection and ascension, when the disciples felt bereft and without their Lord.[8] Though they meet the resurrected Jesus when he appears to them in the upper room, they're restless, and eventually Simon Peter returns to his former life as a fisherman. Some of the others follow, dejected and without purpose. They cast their nets and wait for the fish, but the scaly creatures never appear. The night stretches on without any return on their investment.

In the morning, Jesus stands on the shore and shouts out to them, "Friends, haven't you any fish?" (John 21:5). Was he making a point about fish not being there because the disciples weren't supposed to be fishing in the sea any more, but fishing for people? Yet he doesn't disparage their work either, telling them to put down their net on the right side of the boat. So many fish appear that they can't even haul them into the boat. Simon Peter realizes it's the Lord and jumps into the water, rushing towards him – filled with emotion and impetuous as always. As theologian and teacher Conrad Gempf says in his *Mealtime Habits of the Messiah*, Peter "swims this time; getting to Jesus doesn't always involve walking on water."[9] I love how Conrad opens up this story. Jesus, the king of the universe, is there with his friends, "smoking 'em a few kippers for breakfast."[10] He doesn't condemn them; instead he does something surprising. As Conrad says:

What comes next is the most amazing and gracious thing, and the bit I love the best. Jesus is frying fish. He supplied a miraculous catch. What does he do and say next?

He makes just the right number of fish levitate out of the net and directly into the pan, right? No.

He says, "Have some of these fish already in my pan"?

Wrong.

"Bring me some of the fish I've supplied for you"?

Nope.

Here it is. He says, "Bring some of the fish you have just caught."

Excuse me? The fish *you* have caught? What did *they* have to do with it? By themselves they caught nothing. And it took them the whole night to do it.

Want to know what Jesus is really like? It doesn't get much better than this. He wants us to bring "our" fish, "our" talents, "our" service, "our" faith. Never mind that none of these are "ours" except as a gift. But he's serious. He's willing to regard them as ours; he wants our gifts, generously crediting us with generosity.

Have breakfast with Jesus: BYOF.[11]

We catch fish – and solve mathematical problems and cook gourmet meals and nurse people back to health and teach children and so on – through the fish that Jesus gives us. Amazingly, his resources are ours. Like Jesus said to Peter, he says to us, "feed my lambs." He commissions us to love and create and feed and minister. This is our mandate and joy as Easter people; may we go forth and multiply.

# FESTIVAL TIME

I was wowed the first time I entered the Big Top, the massive tent then used for the teaching/worship sessions for thousands, even though as an American I was used to things done on a big scale.[1] I was a Spring Harvest newbie, taking in the thought-provoking preaching, the powerful singing, the professional organization of this event. But what amazed me more than the music or talks was the scale of this gathering, with so many people from around the country interacting together. We don't have anything similar Stateside. We might have denominational events or storytelling conferences or speakers such as Anne Graham Lotz filling a stadium, but not an event bringing together the intergenerational church to be filled, inspired, and equipped to be salt and light in the local community. I was realizing that although the Christian scene in Britain can feel beleaguered in a way not experienced Stateside, these vehicles for discipleship and growth have blossomed in this setting.

Although I knew Spring Harvest was a huge gathering, I didn't realize just how big until I met a member of the speaking team. When he said that tens of thousands of people attend the various weeks at the two sites, I was humbled to think of God's work over the many years changing lives through this Christian organization.[2] And this is by no means the only such event in these shores. Other constituencies of the British church are served by similarly popular events – New Wine and Greenbelt, Keswick and Detling, and Summer Madness and Soul Survivor and New Word Alive and Youthwork and Big Church Day Out . . .

That first Spring Harvest, we went with our church, as do the majority of people who attend. Nicholas was serving his second curacy in northwest London and a group from the church had long attended, so we joined in. We were glad to share our chalet with another young couple, new friends who would become lifelong companions. Nibbles and drinks with other church members after the evening celebrations cemented relationships as we talked about our day at Spring Harvest and spent time together without any agenda. When Nicholas became a vicar, we went to Spring Harvest again, this time with fifteen-month-old Joshua and our au pair. Our church didn't send a group, so we experienced the conference as a minority do each year – as those who go on their own. It's a much different feeling, especially if you're a parent who shares out the responsibilities of taking care of the kids.

One night the wind whipped the Big Top about and I could feel the chill pervading my insides. During the course of the evening, we were asked to turn to those next to us to chat and pray. I was at the end of the row with several empty seats next to me and no one behind me; the people in front didn't turn around and the few at the other end of the row were immersed in their own group. I suppose I could have tapped the shoulders of the people in front, but I don't know if I'm *that* forward. Among so many thousands I felt the sting of being alone, surprised at my reaction.

The majority of people who attend Spring Harvest go with their churches, which strengthens community – and guarantees you're never sitting at the end of a row on your own, feeling friendless and rejected. That chilly evening has made me more aware of those on their own in such a setting, so I often employ my accent as an ice-breaker. The advent of social media also helps to arrange meet-ups with new mates to share the conference with.

That year with our toddler I started to grasp the huge investment Spring Harvest makes into children and young people. Gathering some of the best in children's and youth workers, they put on programmes that engage the hearts and minds of the kids, from the early-evening all-age worship celebrations to the coolest bands for the 13- to 16-year-olds. For young people who attend a small church, visiting Spring Harvest can open their eyes to the vibrant faith of people across the nation.

When one year we attended Spring Harvest and I was working for a big Christian publisher, I got to experience the coveted Team Lounge. Yes, it warrants capital letters. At that time it occupied a cavernous building, which meant the temperature hovered just above freezing. Old and potentially hazardous heaters crisped up our knees and feet as our backs iced over and I chatted with this author and that. Although I knew these Christian leaders were people just like the rest of us, facing their own challenges, I still felt I had been ushered into a special space. So imagine my surprise and delight when five or so years later I was invited to be a speaker at Spring Harvest. I called Nicholas up to my study and shared the invitation; we were both flummoxed, especially as the email only specified "adult speaking team." I didn't know what role I would play, but was chuffed[3] to be asked.

That year was a whirlwind. The Pyelets nearly burst with excitement as we drove into Butlins, having spotted the white peaks of the Skyline pavilion in the distance. After a stress-free check-in, I made my way to the speaker-briefing session, heart beating faster than normal. I had prepared and over-prepared for the week, and hadn't been surprised when earlier I heard I would be leading the Book Zone – the break-out session with those who wanted to engage with the study material in a book-club setting. I had created discussion questions, mentally ed-ited the theme guide, and was eager to engage in my role.

Lo and behold, the book-club idea flopped. I looked out over the cavernous Whitehall venue, smiling at the first couple of rows of people and glancing back on the rest of the empty chairs. Though book clubs and reading groups are popular for swigging back a glass of your favourite whatever, surrounded by friends while you pontificate over the latest Booker finalist, the format didn't work at Spring Harvest.[4]

I loved my group, however, who came back day after day, having read and prepared, and who enjoyed the small commu-nity fostered in that big space. The spouse of one of the speak-ers said that the Book Zone was the only time she engaged with adults during the day, for otherwise she was the primary parent responsible for childcare. I didn't regret the hours of preparation I had poured into the event, even for the small turnout. It's a cliché, but in God's economy, nothing is wasted.

I didn't know for many years that the best part of Spring Harvest is the early morning session, "The Big Start." Think of the finest all-age service you've ever gone to, multiply that times a hundred, and you've got the Big Start. With gems like the Cathy Madavan–Bob Hartman duo leading the craziness, they usher in truth during the laughs and set us up for the day. I got to sit in on one of their brainstorming sessions once, chortling at their cracks as they went back and forth honing their material. To make something short, meaningful, and funny takes a lot of time and effort.

As I've mentioned, the kids' work at Spring Harvest is amazing, and when Nicholas and I wonder if we should scratch the expense and effort involved in getting us to Butlins, the Pyelets screech at the thought of not attending. Every year, as we drive away, car overloaded with stuff and us all exhausted from too many activities, one of them will pipe up, "I want to go for two weeks next year!"

Surprises await there, such as the year when Jessica had her radio debut. An author-friend was arranging the publicity and asked if my daughter and I would like to be part of the interviews – the view from the punters.[5] Jessica and I got up early that Sunday morning and made our way over to the BBC Bristol van, impressed with the amount of technology they could jam into a small space. The lovely presenter interviewed us outside, wind whipping through our hair, and Jessica was wonderfully articulate. Me, not so much. When asked about why we brought our children to Spring Harvest, I somehow veered into language that made me sound like a cringey Bible-basher. As I heard myself speak I seemed incapable of stopping the drivel coming out of my mouth. Finally, mercifully, I remembered a key pointer when on live radio – you can shut up.

At least Jessica loved the experience; we walked back to the chalet and she said, "I want to be a radio presenter when I grow up! So now I want to be a pom-pom shaker, a vet, and a radio presenter."

The fun isn't limited to the very young. Holiday romances bud at Spring Harvest, or so they tell me – I've only ever attended as a married woman. Jo Saxton has the memory of being a sweet 16 and receiving the attentions of another teenager: "My first kiss! It was Skegness. He was a steward; hot and flirty. We kissed at the end of the week, and stayed in touch till he got a girlfriend!!! It was awesome!"[6]

Another friend, many years after her first kiss, shared how she met her future husband at Spring Harvest after they had been chatting online for six weeks. The online romance continued into embodied life, and they spent their honeymoon at Spring Harvest the following year.

Spring Harvest might evoke memories of first kisses, the cackling seagulls, the specific chill of the bracing seaside wind in early spring, fish-and-chips at the beach, or the plastic-coated mattresses that are so narrow you're sure to fall off of them. But also thousands of voices raised in worship; a bookshop to rival the best online retailer with its breadth and depth; thought-provoking teaching; inspirational activities; and times to recharge and re-energize and generally be amazed at how God is working around the UK and the world. It's not perfect, and it's only one of the many Christian events we enjoy in this country, but I hope it will continue to be one of God's vehicles of grace and discipleship for years to come. Over the years I've come to realize that the British do festivals well – wellies included.[7] If I could, I'd export these events through which the church comes together for inspiring and equipping its people.

# 15

# PLUMBING THE DEPTHS

"They said they'd fixed this," I thought as I peered at the toilet. I was losing a battle with the plumbing at the Strand Palace Hotel on my first visit to London, while at university, and this time I couldn't ask my dad for help. This particular issue had been wafting around for days, with me calling down to reception and them sending someone up to fix the offending bit of porcelain. But it was blocked again. I closed the lid and tried to ignore the sight and smell, wondering what to do.

After breakfast I went to reception, cheeks turning pink as I asked for someone to fix my bathroom.

"Your bathroom?"

I say with embarrassment, "Um, the toilet. It's blocked."

"Oh, certainly. We'll send someone up to mend it."

I retreated to my room, quickly gathering my things for our day at the Old Bailey where we were observing criminal trials as part of my month in London learning about the English legal system.

When I gingerly opened the toilet lid at the end of the day, wondering what I would see, I was relieved to find it clear of anything offensive. But I didn't dare use it for its intended purpose, fearing yet another incident, so when the need struck I made my way to the restrooms[1] tucked away in a darkened ballroom. You may wonder why I didn't ask to change rooms? I was a shy 20-year-old from the Midwest who didn't want to make a fuss.

My first experience with English plumbing came rushing back to me as I read the account of another American, Helene Hanff, who struggled during her first visit to London:

> The shower stall is a four-foot cubicle and it has only one spigot, nonadjustable, trained on the back corner. You turn the spigot on and the water's cold. You keep turning, and by the time the water's hot enough for a shower you've got the spigot turned to full blast. Then you climb in, crouch in the back corner and drown . . . Turned the spigot off and stepped thankfully out – into four feet of water.[2]

At least her shower poured water on her; in centuries past people walking along the street had to watch out for flying sewage. Laws were instituted against the practice of emptying the chamber pot on those in the street below by King Richard II with his writ of *Statuto quo nut ject dung*, "A writ that no one is to dump dung." This was repealed in 1856, with manners taking the place of legislation to warn people of what was to come. They would cry out the pseudo-French phrase, "Gardez l'eau!" which morphed into the pronunciation of gardy-loo, meaning, "Watch out for the water!" And this is where the lovely British slang for the toilet has come from: loo.[3] I guess it's not "Skip to my loo, my darlin'."

Only when I found myself married to my Prince Charming and living in Britain did I discover just how interesting British plumbing can be. Or how cold this country is – even to someone from Minnesota. My home state defines frigid in the winter – we experience temperatures and windchills in the minus double-digit figures, in Fahrenheit – but the buildings stay toasty warm by steady streams of warm air blowing through central-heating vents. Before coming to the UK, I hadn't before felt the unrelenting damp chill that sinks into your bones. The kind that calls for endless cups of tea in the quest to get warm. The summers that pass by with two weeks of sunshine before the rains return. Yet the extended honeymoon cushioned me, those few months of life in a cosy flat in Cambridge student accommodation, complete with a stunning power shower.

And then to Surrey, and to Nicholas's first curacy. Some problems at the church meant we almost didn't live in the house that the church owned. When we visited one of the potential rental properties, Nicholas surprised the church warden by turning on the shower to test it out, seeing if it would be suitable for his opinionated American bride. The shower was more like an Irish mist, in which one would need to jump around in order to get wet, and we were glad when the church finally sorted out the housing issues so we could move into their nicer accommodation. They heeded Nicholas's request and installed a shower for me – better than a mist, but not as good as the White House in Cambridge.

There, in our first home, I came to grips with how clueless I was about English plumbing. For instance, never before had I encountered heat by radiators – to me that was a quaint form of heating in some of the older houses I had visited in Minneapolis. And I certainly didn't know how to work the heating controls buried in a scary part of the kitchen, being mystified by the whole system, not knowing what a boiler was, and leaving the operating of it to my frugal husband. Then an American relative came to visit and squeaked, "Could you please put the heat on?" But Nicholas wasn't home and I felt helpless – the heat came on twice a day, whether or not we needed it.

Next, to northwest London, to Nicholas's second curacy, and a home with single-glazed windows[4] – my vocabulary increasing even more. One morning I asked Nicholas why the curtains in our bedroom swayed back and forth. "Oh, that must be the draught." After about a year, the church removed the original thirties' windows with their art deco design and installed bog-standard double-glazed windows. They were warmer, but not as pretty.

We then moved into our lovely Victorian vicarage in north London that slowly grows warmer each winter, thanks to Nicholas's perseverance and the help of the diocese. Over the years, secondary glazing has been added to the windows.[5] An extra layer of insulation in the loft.[6] New radiators downstairs, and regular cleansing of the system. A new radiator and window for Joshua as we work to get his room allergy-friendly.

I can just about understand bedrooms with basins, such as in our vicarage, but British taps[7] leave me flummoxed. A true mixer tap is a rarity, at least in the old homes I've lived in. Nor do I understand the so-called "mixer taps" that emit two streams of water in parallel, one boiling hot water right next to the cold one. I suppose that's better than the alternative – one tap for hot, and the other, seemingly miles away, for cold.

When early on I asked another American import about this form of plumbing, she said, "I know what you mean. It's partly what you're used to. When my mother-in-law visits the States, she complains that she can never get really hot water out of the tap."

Recently I learned more about the wonderful world of plumbing. Several of our taps needed replacing, the loo needed tweaking, and the shower needed mending. I was chatting to the plumber, asking his opinion about whether oil leaking into the washing drum warranted a new washing machine, when I made a comment about Americans and their opinions about British plumbing.

"You know what's behind that, don't you?" he said.

"I'm not sure – tell me."

"We used to have a law – years ago – that each home could only have one tap off of the mains. So that's why the pressure can be so poor, because it depends on how well it drops down from the loft. Whereas in America, your system has much newer pipes and strong water pressure built right into it."

"So that's why!" I said. "You all are just making the best out of what was regulated by law! I had no idea."

He went on to tell me about the age of many of the water pipes – Victorian, as I knew from seeing the work done on the roads around us – and the effect this has on plumbing.

"No wonder they came up with power showers then," I said. "We don't have them in the States but we never needed them, because the pressure is there in the system already."

In the British mindset, change can be suspect, as I found out when we visited some friends when they were in the midst of remodelling their bathroom. I spied the new sink on the landing with its separate taps and inquired why they wouldn't just go with a mixer tap. The response: "It's what we've always had."

So historic laws and an outdated, inadequate infrastructure are part of what keeps the British from a rousingly good shower.

I wonder, however, how much of the state of British plumbing points to a lurking spiritual malaise. Starting on a grand scale with the world stage, Britain once ruled the world and waves, with its powerful Empire over which the sun would not set. Now it's a small country with yet a big presence – but not the influence it used to wield. Perhaps the sense of being a has-been trickles down into ordinary life – the British don't shape world events like they used to, so what's a bit of annoying plumbing to put up with? Maybe part of the reason is that the adventurous change-seekers left, along with their gene pool, when they founded the New World. I think some of the class system comes into play as well – the feeling that this is our lot in life so we mustn't grumble (whether upper, upper middle, middle, lower middle, or working class – with the uppers not wanting to show off). Or maybe I'm grasping at straws, giving my views from the vicarage, where the house is huge but not our own and we enjoy our taps and shower at the pleasure of the diocese.

British plumbing has shown me that many more factors can influence an ordinary topic than I ever understood when I arrived in Cambridge, not realizing the gift of the shower I enjoyed. Now when I wash my hands in a sink with one tap for hot and the other for cold, I may pause and ponder tradition, history, legislation, and class versus change, convenience, comfort, and expectations.

Time for a long hot soak?

# PART 4
# SUMMER NIGHTS

## 16

# RAIN, RAIN, GO AWAY . . .

Let's talk about the weather. After all, it's a safe topic, and the go-to subject for small talk among strangers or new acquaintances. Though of course I hope by now we're more like friends! As Dr Samuel Johnson said, "When two Englishmen meet, their first talk is of the weather."[1] Island life affords us varied conversation on the topic, for we can experience all four seasons in the space of a day.

I was shielded from the fluctuations of the weather when I first moved here. We planned a celebration of our wedding at the chapel of Nicholas's theological college for Valentine's Day and assumed that the weather in the middle of February would call for the reception in the dining hall. How wrong we were – the day was warm and sunny, like one of those summer-like days we sometimes get in spring. We should have eaten our cake out on the college green.

The sun continued to shine brightly in those early days, so much so that I remarked to one of the long-time transplanted American university lecturers, "It hasn't rained much!" To which he replied, "Just wait."

His statement was prophetic, for after the first six weeks of enjoying the sunshine and watching the clouds march across the sky with a pace I'd never before witnessed, the heavens opened and down it came. It rained. And rained. And rained some more. One day I sat down to write a missive to my friends and family back Stateside and marvelled that during the time I wrote, I witnessed sunshine, a period of clouds, rain, and back to sunshine when I was done. Having lived my life on the massive North American continent, I didn't understand the impact of island life on the weather system.

After my first summer in the UK, I complained to friends and family that I didn't get to partake in summer that year; it never came. Well, it had, but I hadn't understood that the hot, steamy temperatures I was accustomed to in the Washington area were now a thing of the past. I'd go for months without donning trousers when living in northern Virginia – shorts and skirts were the clothing of choice for those hot and humid months. So to pull out a pair of shorts only during the one week of sunshine in the summer months was a crushing change. I see I'm ranting about the weather, and if you're British, you might want to defend your country's weather system. I don't mean to offend. After all, the British weather is character-forming, and we're allowed to mock it gently. Yet now I understand that the British may criticize it, but an American may not, even a British-passport-holding American such as me. And I certainly shouldn't claim that my American weather is superior to yours. Oh my . . . this supposedly safe topic degenerated so rapidly.

Kate Fox in *Watching the English* addresses the all-important issue of the weather. She would say that above I committed the "worst possible weather-speak offence," one "mainly committed by foreigners, particularly Americans, and that is to belittle the English weather. When the summer temperature reaches the high twenties [the eighties in Fahrenheit], and we moan, 'Phew, isn't it *hot?*,' we do not take kindly to visiting Americans or Australians laughing and scoffing and saying 'Call *this* hot? This is *nothing*. You should come to Texas if you wanna see *hot!*'"[2]

According to this sociologist, these types of comments break many unwritten social codes. One is that conversing about the weather eases barriers amongst strangers, which helps the English overcome their reserve, but in doing so those chatting seek to reach an agreement over the state of the weather. Being contrary is not accepted practice when it comes to weather-speak.

My comment above also "represents a grossly *quantitative* approach to the weather," which the English find coarse and distasteful. "Size, we sniffily point out, isn't everything, and the English weather requires an appreciation of subtle changes and understated nuances, rather than a vulgar obsession with mere volume and magnitude."[3]

Coming from Minnesota, I miss snow in the winters. When we enjoy a snowfall here in the UK I'm bemused at the reaction (at least here in the south of England). At the hint of a forecast for snow, people dash to the nearest supermarket to stock up on bread, milk, and water. When the snow comes, London grinds to a halt, often for days. Roads are impassable and cancellations come thick and fast. I daren't drive the car, not because *I* am a danger on snowy roads, but because of all the other drivers out there.

But what I don't understand is why people don't shovel the snow, either in their driveway if they have one, or on the pavement outside their accommodation. My parents never instructed me to shovel as soon as the snow stopped falling, but I guess they didn't need to, for it was an automatic behaviour. If you don't shovel right away, then the snow packs down into, wait for it, ice. Unshovelled pavements and driveways morph into something similar to a skating rink, except people don't generally strap on their skates when going for a quick dash to the high street for provisions.[4]

When we get some snow, I'm delighted. Not only for the beauty of the fluffy or wet white covering, making everything clean and bright, but because I get to wear my Minnesota-approved winter gear and increase my heart rate by shovelling the area in front of the vicarage and the paths around the church.

Nicholas expresses mixed feelings about my snow-clearing antics. Where I grew up not only is it the custom to clear the sidewalks of snow and ice, but the city of Minneapolis deems it law that residents remove the snow within twenty-four hours of the snowfall. Not so in the UK. As Nicholas, son of a solicitor, reminds me, it's the responsibility of our local authority to clear the snow, and if someone shovels and the cleared pavement results in an injury to another, the shoveller could be at risk of legal action. I don't understand . . .

Americans, when thinking of Britain, think not of snow, but of rain and fog. They're surprised when they visit and see the sun shining. And they're stunned if they visit in the summer and we're enjoying a heat wave, short though it may be. But many public places, and most homes, do not have air conditioning, so they remain hot and stuffy during the infrequent heat waves. Cinemas and theatres can be surprisingly warm, especially for an American who reflexively packs a sweater when going to see a film.

I was heavily pregnant one summer during a heat wave of wonderful proportions. Sunshine and heat, and I shivered no more in the vicarage. I loved it, but was surprised by the reaction of my adopted countrypeople. The Britons who had complained so heartily over the rain and mist and lack of sunshine were disturbed by this wild fluctuation in weather. They thought it was too hot, and couldn't imagine how I was holding up, preggers and all.

But heat waves are a rarity in my experience. When we moved into the vicarage, I made plans to enjoy the sunshine, especially with our delightful large garden.[5] I wasn't thrilled about all the green space from a gardening point of view, but rather that now we could finally buy some lawn furniture for lazy Saturdays outside, lolling over lunch in the breeze or relaxing with the paper.

I'll not say that our investment has been a waste, but I've not been able to take the covers off the table or the sunlounger nearly as often as I'd like. Summers so often are chilly, what with that changeable weather that usually includes rain. When friends from California visited recently, they couldn't understand why I insisted we sit outside to enjoy our Pimms,[6] dragging our chairs over to the triangle of waning sunshine. After all, they had perfect weather nearly every day back home – no urgency there. They left the next day and took the sunshine with them; it was a grey, chilly damp excuse of a day in early June, and my friends sent their commiserations from the airport.

But once in a while we land on those rare and perfect summer's days, when all feels right with the world. Maybe we spend that day sharing exquisitely grilled hamburgers and sausages with the ones we love. Or we stroll in the magnificent gardens of a country house. Or we eat and drink by the river at a favourite pub. This, my friends, is bliss.

More common than sunshine is rain, whether a drizzle, dreich (a lovely Scottish word I was taught by a friend to describe the moisture that seems to envelope one), drenching, or downpour.

The weather continues to change, alarmingly. I remember the waterlogged June of the Queen's Diamond Jubilee in 2012, making the impressive flotilla parade down the Thames a soggy affair. Somehow the weather cleared for the Olympics the next month, and by the Paralympics in late August/early September, we baked in the glorious sun.

Then in 2014, we experienced the wettest January since records began in 1910 (a trend that has continued in the years since, with five of the ten wettest weathers occurring in the twenty-first century). Communities were sodden in Somerset; in Devon, the tide even washed away the rail track. Our water stores were full, erasing memories of the drought of a couple of years before with its hosepipe bans (hosepipe – a word I find delightfully quirky) and fears of wildfires. Sitting water and swollen rivers dotted the landscape. We were drenched.

Even the tabloid newspaper, *The Sun*, called for a prayer campaign to stop the rain, saying: "Lord, we've had enough." They published a prayer to the patron saint of weather, St Medard, by Revd Sue Evans, Vicar of St Medard, Little Bytham, Lincolnshire:

Heavenly Father, we are grateful for the gift of water, and in many parts of the world we know people suffer and die for lack of rain.

But dear Lord – we've had enough. We ask you please that the rain may stop soon. We pray for all those people and animals suffering from floods.

As St Medard needed protection from the rain, so now do many people from our land.

For Jesus' sake, Amen.[7]

Which raises an interesting question: Should we pray about the weather? Would the God of the universe intervene with nature – with the systems of weather – in response to the cries of his people? If he does answer these prayers, should we therefore not pray for sunny weekends if we need the rain? I don't hold a clear answer, but I find the subject fascinating. As one who loves prayer, who delights in seeing God break through in our lives, I'm more tempted to take the above questions seriously than not.

When I edited Leanne Payne's spiritual autobiography, *Heaven's Calling*, I learned about praying for the healing of the earth, as championed by Agnes Sanford, for Leanne knew her well. Agnes was a pioneer of the healing-prayer ministry, whom *Newsweek* magazine hailed as one of the six people who shaped religious thought in the twentieth-century. Stirred to pray for the earth, Agnes moved from New England to California to live on the San Andreas Fault. She wrote in *Creation Waits* that the San Andreas Fault is a "rift in the earth . . . subject to disastrous earthquakes."[8] She longed that this rift might "accomplish its work of relieving the tension in the earth's crust quietly, with sufficient small tremors, but without destructive earthquakes."[9] Before coming across the stories Leanne tells in her book about Agnes, I'd never before considered praying for earthquakes to be relieved gently, without great destruction.

When once Leanne visited Agnes and they were praying in Agnes's garden, Leanne remembered with a jolt Agnes telling her about a rattlesnake living out there. She knew that Agnes said it respected her boundaries, but she said to Agnes, "I am definitely not where you are in regards to your snake." But Agnes put her at her ease, and they weren't troubled by the rattlesnake – or the forest fire that burned below them (about which Agnes prayed for rain to come from the nearby Pacific Ocean and, as with Elijah's prayers, the rains came).[10]

Praying for the healing of the earth – I'm aware this might be outside your comfort zone. And it raises hard questions about tsunamis in Haiti, typhoons in the Philippines, earthquakes in Nepal, or other catastrophic weather-related happenings, for I don't want to imply that these natural disasters strike these communities because of a lack of prayer. We live in a fallen world, which isn't as it should be. But I can't help but ponder prayer and the weather. For if God is the Creator, not only of us but of his magnificent earth and planets and skies and seas, and if he made us to communicate with him, wouldn't he want us to pray about that which he's made?

Even if we don't pray for God's ordering of the weather systems, I certainly give thanks when we enjoy the blooms of spring. First come the snowdrops, seemingly earlier every year, the hope of the spring to come. Then the crocuses, orange and purple, spreading joy in their vibrancy. The daffodils break through the mud, the green stalks soon to be covered in a riot of yellows and oranges, swaying in the breeze. And then the tulips and azaleas and rhododendrons, and so on, and so on.

I took my second-ever trip to England in April, a few months into my courtship with Nicholas. I had the trip planned before I'd met him, so I went to his country while he was in mine on his term abroad, and added meeting his family to my itinerary as well as going to Cambridge for the day. My time in Cambridge felt like a dream, framed in the colours of the flowers on the banks of the River Cam. A friend of Nicholas's met me from the station – she an American from Wisconsin, the next state over from Minnesota, who had married an Englishman and lived here a decade. Sara and I hit it off immediately, delving into deep topics as two kindred spirits. She blagged[11] our way onto a free punting trip along the Cam and took me through the gardens of some of the colleges. Although she warned me that life might feel like a shock when I moved over, I hardly took notice. The weather was sunny with a not-too-bracing chill; the daffodils and tulips seemed to define beauty; here was a new friend with whom I connected. As I took the train back to London and reread the card from Nicholas that he wrote for my Cambridge day, I mused that the hype over rain and fog and dreariness was overrated. I would love living here.

And most days I do. The sun shines; the clouds move in; the heavens open. The weather changes all the time, meaning we're not stuck with either too much good weather that we take for granted, or too much that is inclement. I love how a friend puts it: "I once spent six weeks in the Algarve and got so bored with wall-to-wall sunshine that I longed for a day when I could not feel compelled to go on the beach." Indeed, if I wanted continual sunshine, I'd sense a calling to Florida. Time to relax and think about the summer hols (holidays, or vacation time).

# 17

# THE RHYTHM OF REST

Summertime in Britain can feel magical, with dusk settling only long into the evening and the deep greens and other vibrant colours of nature ushering beauty into our lives. Barbecues and afternoon teas in the garden; walks in the countryside; visitors coming to stay; a pub lunch by the river; strawberries and cream; a vicarage without a chill.

Summer can be a wonderful time to build in some rest and refreshment. Schedules slow down in August, with programmes at church halted, kids out of school, work meetings reduced, and expectations of productivity lessened. We can choose to push ourselves more and more, or we can stop and relax. Go on holiday. Take some time in the garden to read and play and chill out. Blow up the paddling pool and splash around with the kids or jump on the trampoline.

We aren't machines; we can't work ourselves nonstop without our bodies crying out in response, whether through headaches or ulcers or more serious complaints. Looking at the creation account in the early chapters of Genesis, we see how integral rest is to us human creatures. We aren't God; we are frail and need the rhythms of work coupled with rest, worship, and play. It's another reason I'm grateful to be living in a culture that hasn't completely lost the ability to take some time off.[1]

Leisure activities can be an area of growth for me and Nicholas, for our preferences vary. But from the start of our marriage, we've agreed on visiting stately homes, such as those belonging to the National Trust or English Heritage. We've viewed the eccentricities of Ickworth in Suffolk with its huge rotunda and wings designed to showcase the first Earl of Bristol's art collection, and have been wowed by the collections of French art showcased in the eye-dazzling surroundings of Waddesdon Manor in Buckinghamshire, home of the Rothschild family. As a recent arrival to these shores, I viewed a classical concert and picnic in the grounds of Anglesey Abbey as a quintessentially English way to spend an evening.

Nicholas's love of history has rubbed off on Joshua. As I've mentioned, starting when he was around 4 years old, he became fascinated with Queen Victoria. His steel-trap of a mind retained many facts about the then longest-reigning monarch, such as the names of her nine children or the date when she died. His love for her was sparked when we visited Osborne House on the Isle of Wight, with its many relics of her family life with Prince Albert. Our son loved seeing the crowded drawing room with a desk for Queen Victoria and one for Prince Albert, littered with photographs, spectacles, letters and books, and trinkets. After the visit to Osborne, Joshua wanted to visit her other royal haunts, so we embarked on a little royal tour. We went to Kensington Palace often enough to get to know the staff, and didn't miss out on her favourite prime minister's country home – Benjamin Disraeli's

Hughenden in Buckinghamshire. A highlight there was the dining-room chair whose legs had been shortened to fit the monarch's diminutive stature. But she grew in other ways; in 2014 a pair of her size 36 pants (underwear) were auctioned off in a bidding war. She would not have been amused. We also journeyed to Windsor Castle and the next door Frogmore House and Mausoleum as well as the Sandringham Estate, the haunt of Queen Victoria's heir, Bertie (King Edward VII).

I find history interesting, taking in the colours, textures, and sights of the surroundings to piece together a picture of how life might have been for those in the elite of society. I don't share the same passion as my menfolk, however, and soon get overwhelmed by the many facts and details of which heiress married which earl in which year. But as with so much of life, we grow to love what those whom we love are passionate about, for hearing them wax on about the history of the Royals or the Second World War enlarges our understanding. As they share their passions, we catch their enthusiasm for their favourite subjects.

Stately homes burst with examples of a prime passion of the British – gardening – taking this pastime to an art form as they till, plant, and weed their beds. Whether the herb or vegetable garden for the kitchen, the walled rose garden, the steamy orangery, or the dizzying hedge maze, these creations welcome us to explore and relax in them.

One of the most famous is that at Hampton Court Palace. We visited it a couple of years ago on a fine summer's day, enjoying the manicured gardens with their riot of colours. But what caught my attention was the Great Vine, planted by Capability Brown in 1768. It's the oldest and largest grape vine in the world; its base is about four metres wide and the vine about forty metres long. And yet it still bears fruit – about 250 to 300 kilos a year. What struck me especially was the ground around the vine, for it was rich and black and seemingly filled with nutrients, yet apparently barren. We were told that they don't allow any weeds or other plants to grow there, as these plants would leech nourishment from the vine.

In thinking about the Great Vine, I remember Jesus' words to his disciples after the Last Supper when he said, "I am the Vine; you are the branches" (John 15:5). Jesus' followers are to cling to and abide in him, drawing nourishment as we seek to remove any weeds that could choke off our life in him. I venture that losing a rhythm of rest and Sabbath could be one of those constricting weeds.

I'm not much of a gardener, but the vicarage has a big space at the back[2] that some years I've cultivated, ripping out shrubs and planting geraniums and petunias in the beds, hanging baskets, and window boxes. (I love petunias, even though I understand that the upper classes see them as a "gaudy bedding plant."[3]) Other summers have passed me by, the flowers that I planted so hopefully in the spring wilting during our times away.

For me, the summertime brings a burst of America, whether through visitors passing through or by us crossing the Atlantic. But the pace of life can increase instead of slowing down if we don't manage the travel and visitors well. Sometimes we err in favour of seeing friends instead of resting, for the former can give us more vitality and energy than a week of afternoon naps. One spring/summer we wondered how so many visitors managed to plan their trips in weekly succession, meaning we had guests every weekend for three months. Feeling we might be overdoing it, I remarked to Nicholas, "Well, we'll have to say no if anyone else asks to come stay." I went upstairs, the speech bubble still hanging in the air, to find a message from one of my favourite people from the Washington, DC, area asking if she and her husband could stop over for a couple of days on their way to Oxford. I laughed – how could we say no?

Journeys back to the land of my birth fill my emotional coffers for the other times of separation during the year. I go shopping with my mom and sister at the Mall of America; my kids join my dad to create watercolour masterpieces in the art studio he built out back; I laugh and reminisce and share with my friends from high school, who have loved me for decades; the kids and I go bowling[4] with my brother; we experience the wonder of one of Minnesota's ten thousand lakes at a family reunion, complete with favourite cousins.

These visits to the States, and the American visitors toting boxes for me of my favourite cereal or chai tea, cause me to mull over the meaning of home. From the start, Nicholas and I defined *home* to be where we live, so early on, when the culture shock seemed overwhelming and I was tempted to "go home," I couldn't. I *was* home.

But early on I often felt homeless, partly because we knew we'd only live for a few months at Ridley Hall in Cambridge where Nicholas was training for ordained ministry. Then his first curacy descended into upheaval not long after we arrived when the vicar was signed off sick, so the question of whether we'd stay or go seemed to cling to us, keeping us from settling. We moved after only two years, to another curacy, which again felt transient as we stayed there another two years for Nicholas to finish his apprenticeship period. Home was where we lived, but rooted we were not. Only when we landed in our first vicarage, having our first child a month later, were we able to create a home for rest, hospitality, and being.

But trips to the States could feel jarring when I thought about home, for I no longer slotted back in to my family's and friends' lives. A missionary states it well:

> When you live overseas long enough, a strange transition takes place. Your "home" country doesn't quite feel like home any more. When you "go home," some of the same people and places are there, but life has moved on in your absence . . . You cannot just pick up where you left off. You are a visitor. An outsider. A guest without a permanent role . . . Some new technology, slang, or cultural trend has become commonplace . . . except for you because you missed it when it first came out . . .
>
> Now that you are home, you are full of experiences and stories from the place that has become your second home . . . But, of course, whatever story you tell them about your host country is hard to relate to. After your quaint tale is done, people go back to talking about the local sports team, the latest in national politics, or something else that you haven't given much thought to in the past few years. It is not that they don't like you. They do . . . But those "back home" people simply cannot relate to your experiences "out there" in that country . . .
>
> Home is no longer home. And sadly, that other place on the mission field will never truly be home either. Home is both places, and neither place, at the same time.[5]

The missionary blogger finishes his post musing on one of my favourite Bible passages, Hebrews 11, about being strangers and exiles on earth. The heroes listed there obeyed God; for instance, Abraham and Sarah followed him to a place they didn't know, which would become not only their home but their inheritance. They held onto the promises from God as being real, even though they couldn't see him. And their faith spurred them on to great things – accomplishments they would never have imagined before the Lord sparked the ideas in their minds.

Whether we're so-called "third-culture kids" (those raised by, say, missionaries who feel torn between their home and host countries) or people who have never left our town, we, like Abraham and Sarah, long for home. We seek to belong. We yearn for acceptance, love, and being known for who we are. So may we find rest for our souls; may we find community where we live; may we express love for and gratitude to the One who calls us home.

# 18

# WHAT'S IN A NAME?

"Oh, you're never supposed to give your name early in conversations," said my fellow American-living-in-London friend. "I was given a copy of *Watching the English*, which explains what's behind it. Mainly a class thing, I think."

She'd lived in the UK for fewer years than I, but she had stumbled onto an area where I'd been making cultural faux pas for ages. I hadn't understood why the British I encountered wouldn't offer their names in polite conversation. My starkest memory of this phenomenon was when I was newly off the boat and meeting a group of spouses of ordinands at my husband's theological college. Sitting in a circle, we formed a cheery bunch, but after they introduced me as the latest arrival, I expected the others to say their names so I might get to know them too. *Nope.*

*Watching the English* helped me understand what's behind this to-me peculiar behaviour. Kate Fox explains the "No-Name Rule" of social situations "where conversation with strangers is permitted, such as a pub bar counter," and how you'd never say, "'Hello, I'm John Smith,' or even 'Hello, I'm John.'" She says:

> In fact, the only correct way to introduce yourself in such settings is not to introduce yourself at all, but to find some other way of initiating a conversation – such as a remark about the weather.
>
> The "brash American" approach: "Hi, I'm Bill from Iowa," particularly if accompanied by an outstretched hand and beaming smile, makes the English wince and cringe . . . The American tourists and visitors I spoke to during my research had been both baffled and hurt by this reaction. "I just don't get it," said one woman. "You say your name and they sort of wrinkle their noses, like you've told them something a bit too personal and embarrassing." "That's right," her husband added. "And then they give you this tight little smile and say "hello" – kind of pointedly *not* giving their name, to let you know you've made this big social booboo . . ."
>
> I ended up explaining, as kindly as I could, that the English do not want to know your name, or tell you theirs, until a much greater degree of intimacy has been established – like maybe when you marry their daughter.[1]

When I read her explanation, I felt an immediate sense of relief touched with poignancy – she named what I had long sensed but didn't understand. I had made many gaffes over the years of being too forward and friendly, but I no longer needed to feel rebuffed or rejected. The English were wincing because of a cultural convention, not necessarily at me personally. Therefore I could still be friendly, and maybe even introduce myself, but now I could gauge how my conversational partner was feeling and whether I dared to break social convention.

Even in the editing of this book I'm learning more about names. My editor gently shared about my cultural misstep at our first meeting at a book launch. She said, "Hi, I'm Jennie," and I replied, "Hi, I'm Amy Boucher Pye." Because I didn't introduce myself generically as "Amy," but as a specific Amy, she immediately thought, "Oh dear, am I supposed to know that name?" Whereas I gave my full name in ignorance, as that's the common custom in my homeland.

I hosted a wide-ranging conversation on the topic of names on my blog and a social media site, heartened by the contributions by the British-living-in-Britain, British-living-abroad, British-who-used-to-live-abroad, Americans-living-in-Britain, and two from other countries.[2]

An English friend who has lived Stateside reckons the no-name rule is a "hang-over from days when you couldn't start a conversation at all unless you had been introduced (think *Pride and Prejudice*). If you're on a train or meeting at the school gates, these days you can break the ice by making some comment about the weather, but that is a sign of two people stuck in awkwardly close proximity, not two people who want to be friends, so introducing yourself does seem a bit forward." She touches on that social structure of class, which again rears its ugly head.

Yet class constraints shouldn't bind people of faith, as she says: "I think it is getting better/more relaxed these days, and it does depend on the situation (so it ought to be better in church – if you're hanging around for a cuppa after the service, that is already a signal that you are seeking social interaction), but I understand that higher up the social scale it is still considered terribly forward to volunteer your name before having been formally introduced. We're just still a bit weird and repressed. But hey, *vive la différence*, eh?"

My extroverted Australian friend felt accepted at church, but knocked against other limiting conventions:

> Because we came to lead a church, we had a built-in 'in' for people's names. However, what I did find in the following few years was that it was not the done thing to bring me to events with their pre-existing friends outside of the church because they were their 'outside of the church' friends (coffee group, mums' group, used to live in the same street group, etc.) and I didn't belong to that group. It was so confusing.

I wonder if this segmentation of friends owes more to how many Christians compartmentalize their lives, rather than an in-built British reserve?

My heart went out to a fellow expat who added, "Maybe this is part of the reason why it's so difficult to make friends here. People will say hello if you say it first, well, most of them will, but you may have chatted with them in the street for weeks or months and they certainly do not want to come in for a cuppa! Keep your distance, please! Why don't people want friends? I thought that was a universal need! I'm from Norway and have no family; it does make me feel isolated."

That gap between saying hello and actually forming a friendship can feel like an unbridgeable one, and I don't fully understand it. We all need friends; her comment reminds me of my deep loneliness when I had just arrived in the country and I asked God for even one friend. Perhaps out of a fear of too little time or other issues of rejection we subconsciously put quotas on our friendships.

Whether introducing ourselves in the hope of friendship or merely making polite conversation, one expat seems to have the no-name social convention sussed:[3] "I've found that as long as I don't accompany any introduction with overly friendly tones or too loud a voice, I haven't committed too many cultural faux pas. Or at least that I know of. Best to act slightly embarrassed, even if you don't feel it."

I wonder how she'd be without any social constraints: "I'm just aware that even after three years in the UK and seven in Canada, deep down, I'm still the American cheerleader I used to be. That's a bit much for anybody."

I can resonate with the feeling of being a bit too much for people – and I'm no cheerleader. This sense of needing to hold back can exacerbate a lack of confidence that might already be lurking inside, as it was with me. For instance, when I worked for a big publishing conglomerate in London, we in the religious books division were invited to a drinks reception with staff from several other arms of the company in the office of my boss's boss. I stood at the door, eyeing the conversations but staying glued to the spot, seemingly unable to enter. As one of my colleagues arrived she asked me if I was going in, but I smiled and turned away. I guess I lacked sufficient emotional resources that day.

This sometimes crushing, sometimes hampering, lack of confidence can keep me quiet as I refrain from giving my name or voicing my opinion, or can make me couch any comments with ifs, ands, or buts. Yet my journey to finding myself in Christ, and in Britain, has entailed me finding my voice as

I step into the meaning of my name – beloved. As with all children of God, this is my central identity, born out of the never-ending love of him who made us and knows us and calls us by name. His love defines our existence.

So when I take on the moniker Too Much or Too Little, I learn to train myself to turn to God and ask him how he sees me. As I wait for his loving word, I sense his gentle whisper in my spirit that I'm Enough. When a British acquaintance lets me know with cutting humour that I've overstepped cultural conventions, and that I'm Not Allowed, I can take the pain of the biting irony to God and ask him to remove the sting. He shows me that I'm Secure, for in him my soul finds rest, and he is my rock and salvation.[4] Or when I'm introduced as "the vicar's wife," with any loaded meanings, I know that I'm Cherished – Amy who is married to Nicholas, mother to Joshua and Jessica.

How about you? Do you call yourself Worrier? Worthless? Ugly? As we look to God, asking him how he sees us, we hear his nudges of grace, sensing that no longer are we Worrier, but we are Warrior. No longer Worthless, but Priceless. No longer Ugly, but Beautiful or Handsome.

I've met a couple of women who have changed their names. One chose the name of a flower for her new name, leaving behind her given name because it brought up memories of an abusive mother. She felt that she couldn't live the new life if she had to keep that old handle. Another's Christian name meant "bitter," and she changed it to Hannah, which means grace. She hadn't been defined by abuse, but rather experienced a low-level feeling of disease and a dislike for the name she had to answer to. She took action at a ministry conference, crossing out her name on her name tag and christening herself anew.

Jesus in his letters to the seven churches speaks of the new name he has for each of his people. He says in Revelation 2:17: "Whoever has ears, let them hear what the Spirit says to the churches. To the one who is victorious, I will give some of the hidden manna. I will also give that person a white stone with a new name written on it, known only to the one who receives it."

I love the imagery of the white stone. One meaning relates to an admission ticket, for in the ancient world, people used pebbles for admission to events – in this case, for a messianic banquet. The white stone says that we're welcome and invited to the banquet; we're not losers who are left out and rejected. This meaning also hearkens to Jesus' parable in Matthew 22 of the wedding feast, when the servants go out into the streets and invite the good and the bad when the invited guests don't show up.

Another meaning of the white stone has to do with jurisprudence, for in some ancient courtrooms, the jurors would cast a white stone for acquittal and black for conviction. So with the white stone, Jesus says that he's the judge over what the Pergamum Christians suffered, and that God is giving them a "yes" vote. We're acquitted and not convicted, for by Jesus' blood we are free.

Or the white stone can symbolize purity – our sins are washed away, and we are clean. Or eternal life, for in heaven, we won't be marred by sin and shame. We will live completely out of our new self, with our new name blazoned for all to see.[5] Our new name is one of splendour, for we are a royal diadem in the hand of God. No longer are we deserted or desolate, but those in whom the Lord delights. We will be joined with our bridegroom, for our Lord will call us his beloved and will rejoice over us with singing.[6]

# 19

# QUEUING, AND OTHER BRITISH SPORTS

I nearly missed the ceremony.

It was the end-of-term presentation for the multi-sports club that Joshua attends. Each child receives a small medal for participating, but three children are awarded trophies – those for best sportsperson, most improved, and best all-rounder. Several years previously, Joshua had received the best sportsperson trophy, but in his mind that seemed long ago. I wanted to show him love and support, and in the spirit of soccer moms across America, I knew when it came to the medal ceremony my heart rate would elevate, either to celebrate with him or mask any disappointment.

My time was waning and Jessica and I were cutting it close to make it to school for the ceremony, but issues of interior plumbing and the choosing of toys were holding us up. We finally got there and walked into the hall to see George, the wonderful leader, handing out the medals to each of the kids.

He was halfway through, but Joshua was the last child in the line, so we hadn't missed out.

Then George announced that he was giving out the bigger trophies. The first was for best sportsperson, and it went to a little Japanese girl who seemed very sweet. I looked at Joshua to gauge how he was feeling, for I reckoned that trophy was his best shot. Inwardly I thought, "Maybe next year."

George then said that the next award went to the most improved. He said how this person had made great strides over the term, and that he was impressed with how well they were doing and the gains they had made over the months. He said, "And this award goes to . . . Joshua!"

I shouted out, "Woo hoo!" and clapped for joy. The parents around me looked at me, slightly askance that I would be so vocal in my response. I had tossed aside any acquired British reserve, for in that moment I wanted my son to know how proud I was of him. He received the award and sat looking down, appearing deeply moved.

Afterwards I went up and gave him a huge hug, and we asked George to have a photo taken together. I said to Joshua, "I hope I didn't embarrass you. I was just so excited! Well done! I'm so proud of you!"

Later he told me that he had almost cried when he received the award, he was so happy, but that I had embarrassed him, for the other parents hadn't shouted out like that.

"True," I responded. "You know, the Japanese parent wouldn't be loud like me, for in their culture they tend to be reserved and respectful." I asked if Daniel, who received the best all-rounder trophy, had a parent there, and he said no.

"Well there you have it," I said. "You have an American parent, and sometimes Americans can be loud and enthusiastic. That's just how it is, my dear!"

I think secretly he enjoyed my outburst.

At times I can let rip in full American spirit, especially when it's for a son who overcomes his physical challenges to persevere and achieve. But his comment about this not being socially acceptable makes me take pause. Yes, we shouldn't laud our children's achievements at the expense of other children, but shouldn't we celebrate and uphold them when they've done something great? A little loosening of that British stiff upper lip wouldn't hurt.

But that's just not done, as my "fully fledged Swim Club Mum" friend observes. Her daughter swims competitively, and with all the training and competitions she can spend sixteen hours or more a week at the pool. She says:

> Yes, a little gentle cheering is fine, as long as one doesn't go too over the top, and as long as you also cheer for the offspring of those you're sitting with. If several children that you know are in one race, best to cheer on the team, 'Come on, [insert team name]!'
>
> One Swim Club Mum shrieks like a banshee when she cheers her son on and that is widely considered in poor taste. While nobody would say anything, they wince. Also, the words you shout do matter; 'Come on!' and the child's name is ok, but some parents bellow things like, 'Give it to 'em!' and 'Have it!' and attempted coaching, like 'Legs! Legs!' and so on, and they get the odd disapproving glance as well.
>
> Since my daughter has confirmed that she can't hear a single thing while she's going like the clappers in the water, I tend to

clap and shout 'Well done!' or 'Hooray!' when she's finished and give her thumbs up when she glances my way. I have learned many lessons about Swim Club politics in the last year.[1]

Social rules of proper behaviour and fair play seem to be at work here; no garish displays of loud emotion allowed, because children with vocal parents shouldn't be seen to be valued more highly than those with parents showing restraint. Call me over-enthusiastic, but if I was investing that much time into watching my offspring train and compete, I think I'd find it hard not to emulate the mother who shrieks like a banshee. At least the fellow parents could chalk it up to me being "that loud American."

Before moving to the UK, I never watched tennis. A couple of my friends were tennis nuts, but I didn't understand the game, nor the attraction. I listened to their stories about travelling to New York for the US Open or their dreams about a round-the-world trip for the Grand Slams, but I remained unmoved. Then I moved to England. My first summer here I mused:

> We watched Wimbeldon [nope; I couldn't spell] a bit, which I've actually started to enjoy. I've never watched tennis before, so I was learning the rules. It was good to watch with people, as they could explain different things, like "Advantage Agassi" and "Deuce" and "Breakpoint." Two Americans won (Sampras and Davenport)!

It's been a journey of years, but I love tennis now, and especially Wimbledon. It might have something to do with the fine BBC coverage with its corresponding lack of adverts,[2] but partly it's a sport I've taken to through the passion of Nicholas and his commentary during the matches. It's uncanny how he'll utter something about one of the players – related to tactics or history – and a moment or two later one of the (professional) commentators will say the same thing.

When I learned that the opportunity to buy tickets to the grand event could be won through the public ballot, I duly entered and was floored a few months later when we received notification from the All England Lawn Tennis and Croquet Club that we were welcome, for a price, to attend the men's semi-finals day. Andy Murray lost that day, but what a highlight to experience the atmosphere and surroundings. Seeing Sue Barker, Tim Henman, and John McEnroe chatting before the matches, cameras trained on them, reminded me that this was happening live, broadcast around the world. Centre Court appeared so much smaller in real life than on television.

We were at a friend's fiftieth birthday party when tennis history for Britain was made. In 2013 the nation's 77-year wait for a new British men's champion ended when Andy Murray was crowned victor. We had seen him succeed at the London Olympics the year before, but the elusive title seemed out of his reach until the unthinkable happened and he actually won. Fred Perry, you can rest in peace, for finally there is a new male British champion.

My son and husband share a secret language. Not secret by design, but by default, as Jessica and I don't understand out of a lack of interest. First thing in the morning I'll hear wafts of overs, runs, and "268 for 8" if Joshua has been listening to the radio to catch up on the cricket matches being played in different time zones. My menfolk love to take the bus for a day at Lord's cricket ground;[3] they adore keeping each other up to date on all the latest happenings, whether for England or other teams around the world. I may have grown to love tennis through sharing Nicholas's passion, but cricket is not a sport I've been won over to. But I'm glad that father and son share this bond, not only of football (although they support different teams) but especially with cricket. For the family influence of a love for sports can last a lifetime.

Only recently I learned what is behind the odd name of the series between England and Australia – "The Ashes." There's a particularly strong rivalry between the two countries when it comes to sports, as I've gathered over the past few years by working for an Australian company. Back in 1882, Australia finally triumphed over England, as MV Hughes outlines in her 1927 guide to England, "chiefly owing to the demon bowling of F.R. Spofforth." She tells how the *Sporting Times*, a weekly English newspaper, published a self-deprecating "In Memoriam" notice:

> In affectionate remembrance of English Cricket, which died at the Oval on 29th August, 1882. Deeply lamented by a large circle of sorrowing friends and acquaintances. R.I.P. (N.B. – The body will be cremated and the ashes will be taken to Australia.)
>
> The next match was in Australia, when the English team was victorious. Some Australian women then burned a stump, put the ashes in a small wooden urn and gave it to the conquering team as a trophy.[4]

I now smile when I hear about the Ashes, knowing its quaint history, but with cricket overall, I must lack the necessary nuance. I can't find it satisfying to devote five days to following the ups and downs of a match and have it end in a draw. Or maybe I fall into the category of lacking smarts, for according to a friend, "Cricket is baseball for intelligent people."

When I asked Nicholas why football[5] is the main sport of the UK, he said, "It's a working-class game – all you need is a ball and a bit of grass. Whereas cricket is a gentleman's game – you need equipment. In fact, in the past there used to be a cricket match for 'the gentleman versus the players' – the toffs versus the working class." I responded, "You mean sports are segregated by class distinctions too? Groan."

I didn't know the Christian influence on football's formation until Nicholas told me about an article in *Christianity* magazine published prior to the 2010 World Cup. According to the writer, in Victorian times the church was widely involved in the lives of young people, with 85 per cent of children attending Sunday school. With people moving from farms to cities, but living in small houses, they looked for places of leisure, and often the pub won out. Also, the work week changed down to five and a half days, meaning that men often went straight to the pub after the Saturday morning shift. As a way to prevent violence, stop drunkenness, and engage the many young children in a positive pursuit, many clergy became involved in setting up football clubs, their matches starting at 3 pm on a Saturday. By the 1870s, 25 per cent of the football teams had a church affiliation.[6]

I wonder what those Victorian clergymen would think of the Beautiful Game now, such as how it seems to have become a religion in its own right. Yet this isn't new, as MV Hughes reflected when the Football Association was only about forty years old. She said that although religion is confined to certain days and places in this country, "sport in any form is sacred."[7]

Indeed, football fanatics abound, whether the fans who travel to all the matches, here and abroad, or those like Nicholas who plan their social calendar according to the World Cup fixtures. Football provides a club whose members exhibit heartfelt devotion to their teams, with fellow fans forming a strong community.

I pinched myself during the summer of 2012. To be in London for the Diamond Jubilee and the London Olympics felt magical. The sports-mad Nicholas said he'd rather watch the events on television than go to any of them, but I was keen to soak up the atmosphere and to make fun memories with the kids. I had tried for tickets in the public ballot, not succeeding in scoring any to the Olympic Park but managing to take Joshua to fencing and Jessica to table tennis at other venues. Clad in a mixture of stars-and-stripes and the Union Jack, and waving both flags, we found it fascinating to watch athletes at the top of their sport. We enjoyed seeing them fight it out for a medal through their tactics, elite physical conditioning, and strength of will.

I was determined to take the kids to the Paralympics so that we could visit the Olympic Park. And although at first I wondered if the Paralympics might feel second best as we didn't know any of the athletes, I soon changed my opinion when we saw the grit, determination, and perseverance of those who have overcome daunting challenges. We sat in the steamy aquatics centre, inspired by the swimmers' speed and skill, and on another day slapped on the sun cream while watching the athletes run and cycle in the Olympic Stadium.

I found it fascinating during the Olympics and Paralympics to witness the seemingly immovable British reserve melt away. Londoners welcomed the world brilliantly and I especially enjoyed chatting to strangers on the Tube without making anyone feel uncomfortable.

London 2012 was a resounding success, from the quirky and inspiring opening ceremony (with the awe-inducing entrance of Her Majesty with Mr Bond) to the quality of the venues to how the military stepped in to provide support when the government deemed the level of security inadequate. It seemed like time was suspended as the British believed in themselves, realizing that not only could they put on a very fine event but they could bring home a swarm of medals too.

We can't leave this chapter without addressing the art and sport of queuing. After all, if it was an Olympic discipline, the British would bring home the gold year after year. Some people reckon the importance of forming an orderly queue came about during and after the Second World War, when rationing meant waiting for daily provisions and shared hardship entailed pulling together out of support and respect. The British value of fairness comes strongly into play as well.

Though queuing seems to be innately formed in the British character, it's not appreciated around the world, as a British expat woman living in the Netherlands recounts. She tells of her despair when getting to the bus stop first, standing in an obvious place for the others to fall behind her, and yet how those latecomers push ahead onto the bus – meaning she doesn't get a seat and has to stand, weaving from side to side for the forty-minute journey. Although she employs some tutting, sighing, and head shaking, her signals are lost on the Dutch. Whereas a tut in a queue in Britain would send the perpetrator scurrying back to the end of the line, red-faced and ashamed.[8]

When it comes to sport, you may love or loathe it, but here in the UK its importance can't be overstated. I tried for many years to ignore sport – cricket and football especially – but I'm learning that when someone you love finds it so marvellous, it's best not simply to tolerate it, but to laud their passion and celebrate their victories as your own.

## 20

# PARALLEL LIVES

One summer, I slept in another woman's bed, drove her car, used her Wi-Fi, watched her television, and ate breakfast at her table. And she mine. We swapped homes with Jo and Chris Saxton, who are British but who have been called to America, living in such wonderful places as California, Arizona, and Minnesota. They're based a few miles from the home where I grew up, and where my parents still live. They have been church planters, and Jo is a speaker, writer, leadership coach and all-round visionary person.[1] The time in their home felt surreal in some ways, as if I was entering a parallel universe: This Could Be Your Life.

Join us as we plot and plan:

**22 July**
**Jo:** hey amy! can't believe we nearly swap! house is unbelievably untidy – but now everything is getting out of the way – including the dog tomorrow – I am free to blitz it! Has the heat wave gone?

**Amy:** Hey there! I know; so soon. I'm slowly getting the house sorted, but we had a dead bird in the fireplace in our bedroom! Dis-gust-ing. Heard its claws scratching and ended up sleeping in the guest room. Heat wave should be gone by the time you come. But not as chilly as it can be – highs in the low 70s I think. I love the heat but feel bad for the older people. You'll be here for some of the buzz of the royal baby . . .

**23 July**

**Jo:** Are you at the airport yet???

**Amy:** Us? No. We leave on Thursday morning! When do you arrive? Kids still have school tomorrow!

**Jo:** School!!!!!!!!!!????? No!

**Amy:** You've forgotten school in late July!? I wonder if we'll each have a bit of "this could be your life" déjà vu during this house swap!

**Jo:** i bet we will. Final clean up and pack. Oh. The. Madness!!!

**25 July**

**Jo:** LOVE your home!!! Thanks so much; already massive blessing to us. So far I've stood looking at your bookshelves feeling spoilt for choice. And oohing and aaahing at your kitchen. Also forgot to buy you toilet roll. Soz.

**26 July**

**Amy:** You made it! We made it too! Yes, we love our home, but I'm sure the shower (which is a POWER shower nonetheless) is nothing compared with yours.

And oh my. If I lived in America I would have storage. And an en suite. Your house is fab and so clean! This will be amazing to be in your home – to have our own space, and to see my family. Sleep, please come to us soon. Hope you guys cope with jetlag. Enjoy!

**Jo:** Jet lag is a trip, isn't it? We were all hanging out about 4 am. Hey, loved the devotional today re John Stott. Now I've got some time and space to hear the yes or no of God!

**Amy:** Thanks so much! Good to remember to take time to be quiet and with God while here. Temptation is to submerge into family stuff. Hope you're loving London and that sleeping in the heat hasn't been too much of a shock.

**27 July**
**Amy:** [After a lot more back and forth, led by me] PS I will leave you alone now!

The following came to me this morning: jet lag is the body's way of saying that it's not used to a new time zone yet. Functions of sleep and waste removal take time to move over to the new system. So, too, has my mind needed to adjust. The daily emails to Jo have been a way of letting go of London and embracing Minnesota. But the sacrament of the present moment means I need to stop the emails and live here in the now. Not looking over my shoulder at that life, but living the one here, for this time and place.

It goes back to place again. Being rooted where I am, even during a holiday. Switching off takes time, and intention. Being thankful for being here. The sacrament of now.

**Jo:** I know exactly what you mean – the first few days were great for the transitions; it really helped me too to be honest, but yes there's the now to face and embrace with God. So enjoy the next few weeks!

A few years before our house swap, I went on a retreat, and out of the blue felt strongly that God was calling me to relinquish my desire to move back to the States. I had been on a campaign to move back – and Nicholas had even interviewed for a church in Virginia, but after the interview we both knew it was wrong. Starting off my retreat and hearing, "Give up your campaign," was not what I welcomed. I closed my journal in a huff and spent the rest of the time reading spiritual books – running from God's gentle but firm nudge.

But I heeded that whisper, kicking and screaming along the way, wondering if relinquishing a move meant I'd never again live close to my parents or other family members and friends. Over the months, as I gave my feelings to the Lord, I asked him to help me live in the present and not long to be elsewhere. It took a series of acts of the heart, but acts in practice too. For instance, I finally bought the bookcases I had been putting off purchasing because I hoped we'd be moving overseas, and I welcomed as a gift the expensive food mixing machine that I knew couldn't work in the States because of the different voltage.

The transformation took place slowly – but it did occur. So much so that when Jo and I swapped houses, I was still rooted back in London, logging onto social media sites almost obsessively to see what was going on at the vicarage and in the lives of my friends. And in messaging back and forth with Jo, as the extracts above show.

But that early morning, awake with jetlag and sitting on Jo's sofa, I understood that I needed to be present where I was, there in the land of my birth, with my family around me. I realized that God *had* changed my heart since that retreat, and although I still harboured longings to live in America, now they didn't cripple me from engaging in my life in London. My act of relinquishment had been God's loving but firm direction to help me enjoy the gift of living in the present. Now that I was Stateside, again I needed to focus on where I was, and with whom.

So after that a-ha moment, I slowed down the social media chats and asked God to wake me up to the pleasures of America. And he did. Our summer was amazing, not least for the time in Minnesota, but also during our epic road trip from Minnesota to Washington, DC, and back, which gave my British family a taste of the wide open spaces, rolling fields, family diners, and friendly faces of the land of my birth.

We learned and loved that summer, immersing ourselves in people, nature, and museums. I found myself learning more about America and Americans through the eyes of my foreign-born husband and children. Some things were on a superficial level, such as my surprise that one of the children's favourite activities each day was to run across the (not busy) street to retrieve the mail out of the mailbox. Or how when we'd be driving they would point out the foreign-looking fire hydrants, or that Nicholas would notice that there were no fences (and certainly not hedges) dividing neighbours, and he wondered why there weren't any pavements[2] around.

Having Jo's home to settle in made me consider the differences between the two countries as well. Again, many things were on a surface level, such as the ease of having a cutting board incorporated into the kitchen cabinets, which slid neatly in and out like a drawer. Or garbage disposals – so convenient, just rinse that plate and down goes any uneaten food, no stinky compost to give another thought to. Or the ubiquity of tumble dryers, which make for easy laundry days – but again, what about hanging out the laundry to catch the breeze and smell so nice and fresh? Admittedly, some communities have rules about not hanging any clothes outside, because it "mars the landscape."

Also when Stateside I noticed free dog poop bags in a Minneapolis park, wondering who financed such largess. Or when I saw removable cushions on the chairs in the shopping centre, I mused how those wouldn't last long in London. But I also sighed as I got into the car every time I wanted to go somewhere – a quick walk to the shops simply isn't possible because of the sheer size of suburban and rural areas.

Deeper things we noticed had to do with the disposition of people, such as the general openness and friendliness of those around us. Especially in Minnesota, for there's a saying that characterizes them – "Minnesota Nice." One day when on our road trip, Jessica and I were using the loo in a McDonald's when a couple of girls a few years older than her started chatting to her. My daughter sees only friends, not strangers, so she immediately engaged in the conversation with verve. When we got into the car, she said with wonder, "Those girls were so nice!"

I didn't want to make a big deal about differences in cultures, but the incident got me thinking about how the immigration experience has shaped the growth of a nation. The names of towns and cities may reflect the places from where the immigrants came – Dundee, Monroe, Toledo – but a new people emerges with its own identity in a new land. If you're all immigrants, the class system of old doesn't bind you, especially if you're a rag-tag of outcasts like in America. According to the nation's lore, you can be who you want to be, whether a self-made businessperson, entrepreneur, chef, teacher, writer, or whatever. This friendly can-do spirit, open to change and new possibilities, I find appealing.

Jo and I picked up our conversation later, at a gentler pace, talking not only about surface things like how to set out the recycling but about deeper topics such as church life, social class, and relationships.

### 6 August

**Jo:** Ah the UK – I love it, I do – really enjoying here. But I miss the States. And I know it's where the kids call home – though they LOVE being here. I even listened to Springsteen the other day – "Dancing in the Dark." I NEVER listen to Springsteen. I just decided I'm weird and laughed it off.

That said, it's a rich time here. I love English spirituality that we're reconnecting with – Soul Survivor and New Wine have been fantastic. Not so much the charismatic stuff – I can get that in my living room. I mean the kind of church which is not used to being the centre of a culture/that isn't popular and all that . . .

The differences in church life struck us both as we moved between the two cultures. Big church/small church/neighbourhood church/missional communities – they all have their positives and challenges. I came away from the conversation thinking it's a call to "bloom where you're planted," for no church will be perfect.

**7 August**

**Amy:** Churches – I know what you mean. We've been part of a neighbourhood church for a decade plus now. I don't even know what big-church life looks like any more. Was in a massive one in Northern Virginia, but because it was Anglican it was different than, say, an evangelical free church. So my take on church in the UK comes from the view of something a lot smaller than a New Wine church or conservative evangelical one like St Helen's Bishopsgate.

Neighbourhood church can feel tough – committed Christians are like gold dust, and can be overworked. They feel pressure to step up to the plate for children's work or giving financially or the welcome team – because there aren't enough volunteers to go around. I see them some weeks (and can feel this myself) looking weighed down and beleaguered. Is this the "victory" we're supposed to be living? Where's the joy? Where's the Harvest, Lord, that we keep praying for? I don't blame people for going to the huge churches, especially if they have kids whom they want to see on fire for God. Community, quality kids' and youth work, great preaching and music – big church can deliver.

And yet I've seen joy in the neighbourhood church. Deep friendships, born out of prayer. Sparks of life and God's work in bringing life and faith and joy. Is it worth it? Yes. Is it hard? You betcha.

**9 August**

**Jo:** Since coming back home to Minnesota, what I miss, weird though it sounds, is living in a place where Christianity isn't the subculture. I realized it was nice being away from the Christian industry most of all, but there's an intensity about Jesus that I miss — whereas here I feel I'm listening or reading people's conversations and thoughts and opinions on things that don't seem to matter now, if they ever did.

And I love big churches, but I'm glad we've planted into a smaller one. It's hard not to be defined by what you get out of church when so much is put on for you. Church planting comes with a whole different set of expectations, especially as we are bi-vocational right now. You can't rely on the vicar/pastor/whoever as everyone gets to play — we're a community of everyday missionaries. And I thought the kids would suffer for it, but they love it, being more involved and knowing more people.

I don't miss the big church vibe. I love it as a conference that lasts for a few days, but it's very hard to sustain as a way of life. It's harder to build community and share lives; it's hard to know people and feel known. And I think if we're meant to give our time to being agents of change in the world, it possibly means spending less time in churches . . .

Our global lives, not only between the US and UK, but with Jo's roots in Nigeria, made the topic of friendship — what it looks like, how to sustain it — one we could devote a whole book to.

**12 August**

**Jo:** As you well know, seeing your friends – the people who truly know you, and have done for a long time – that's pretty special. I'm beginning to wonder if friends like that can ever be replaced – whether you can have the time or opportunity to build the same depth of friendship as those you have with people from your childhood/college/young adult years. I'm sure it's exacerbated by the moving around we did in the US, but it's taking a long time to grow friendships there . . .

**Amy:** The friendship thing is really interesting. This trip I'm hearing how hard it can be to make friends in Minnesota in particular, partly because of the influence of the German/Swiss/Norwegian/Swedish heritage. People get their friendships really early and then as they age don't move around so much, and don't look outside themselves to welcome others in.

These are big generalizations, of course, and having said all of that, my friends from high school are welcoming, outward-looking people. They're incredibly special to me, partly because one of our best friends died when she was 19, so that bonded us together for life. Yet I know in Minnesotans, the northern European influence can mean a lack of demonstrable emotions, which can appear cold to outsiders.

But I don't know if I totally agree about the generalizations I hear about British/American friendships, that Yanks are fast friends who will then leave you while Brits are slow to become friends but then will stay your friend for life. I've stayed friends with some people in each of the churches that we've been part of here, but some I've let go. Some friendships were broken because of conflict, and one in particular hurt me deeply. Is it more personalities than national characteristics?

**14 August**
**Jo:** I've found local friendships quite difficult here. But I don't think that is about the underbelly of "Minnesota Nice," I think it's had a lot to do with me being a pastor and a pastor's wife in a mega-church (with a celebrity complex). I think people assumed they were a burden or assumed I was more spiritual than I am. That made it hard to make a deep connection. Also a lot of people here had known each other for years, and they were raising families – who had time to add a new friend anyway? They had all the friends they needed. I also think I'm a little bit loud for the Minnesota world!

For me it seems timing, personality and context are the key factors in my friendships.

Timing – My twenties were formative and we were a large young adult community in my church – and we had the time to be together. Then there were some friends I made in Arizona when my girls were babies and we were moms with babies the same age. Then there were my friends in California who met at the school gate when our kids started kindergarten. They in their own way were seminal moments; friendships forged around something. Now I'm a working mom with a busy life and I travel for work – I sometimes wish for those deep friendships that could be sustained in these thin seasons where there feels like there is no time.

Personality – That said I think this counts for a lot. I am not a girly girl. I am the ENTJ, Enneagram 8 – all the personality type/traits that say I'm a cold-hearted shoreline, or dominating, or heartless, etc. And I am and I'm not those things. I'm intense and I'm driven and so I'm drawn to friends like that or to people who don't mind me being like that! I'm more likely to bond over the Harvard Business Review than a recipe, even though I enjoy cooking. I don't know whether Americans move on – I think I do! Physically as well as emotionally. That said I've been surprised at how few of my US friends have even attempted to stay in touch when we've moved.

Context – But that said I do have some rich friendships – and now you've got me thinking about them, I'd say the friends here and beyond have been people whom I've gone through STUFF with. So the friends I do have from here suffered last year with me, and that fashioned our friendship. And when I look back on the friendships that mattered – American or Brit – they've all had a moment where we've been through the fire, and that's what made it feel safe and known . . . they're my people.

I think I've also accepted some of my friendships are simply global. There are some people I try to see annually. There are others I text as though they live in the States. So I think I've come to terms with it, stopped grieving what I've lost and started being thankful for technological advances that keep me connected.

**Amy:** A Brit loud in America – love it! I know what you mean about friendships when one leads a church, or is married to a church leader. Even with my closest friends, there's always a layer that I can't share; that feeling which might be small, but is still there. Having said that, I have a group of women at church who will be my friends for life. We met together weekly for prayer during some rough seasons, and the resulting love and depth of commitment to each other is a wonderful gift. The seasons of strife sucked, but we all grew in character and faith. I can be fully myself with them, and I love that we can do daily life together – seeing each other on the school run or on a Sunday morning.

That hooks in with what you were saying about how friendships grow through trials. We take off the masks and let people in to our deepest parts – the most vulnerable – when we're facing the horrors of death or betrayal or accidents or abuse or disease or disappointment. Supporting our friends during these times is a massive privilege I try not to take for granted. And being loved by them when I'm going through the trial is what makes it feel possible to take life's next step. I guess it goes back to us being God's hands out there in the world, as Jennifer Rees Larcombe says. He spreads his love in and through us.

So I agree that although personality and seasons and context all shape one's friendships, those deep, rich, soul-mate type friendships are often birthed in the valleys of life.

Later in September, after we both were back in our homes, I asked Jo about some of the characteristics of living in America, which started with the ease of life in that big country but morphed into a conversation about class and opportunities and national outlooks:

**Amy:** What about convenience and the American way? Do you get tired of driving everywhere? Wish you could take a walk up the high street? Take for granted things like a garbage disposal and the cheap cost of stuff at Target and that fabulous amazing shower you have downstairs (and two loos upstairs; be still my beating heart)? I don't know how I would handle being able to visit Target every week if I lived there. Now when I go I splurge, and the kids know they can say I want this and I want that, and usually I buy it – to put away for birth-day/Christmas presents. We splurge and buy and, yes, I love it. But I also know I'm only there a week or two; the buying has to stop when I get home to England because I hate paying That Much More for stuff here.

**Jo:** I often contend that if I still lived in England I would be slimmer. I would walk more, I would eat less junk, eat more at home and have a less sedentary life. If nothing else the temperatures would be more amenable than my years in sun-scorched Arizona or the frozen tundra that is Minnesota. I think I would be slimmer. But then maybe I am dreaming!

I LOVE the convenience for the most part – Target is my second home and I know the staff well because I'm there so often – it's my one-stop shop; it's like a village. And I'm happy for it to raise me and my children. I feel we're spoiled with the space and the two cars and it's a bit embarrassing to consider the cars necessities. And yet in America where we live, we couldn't do life with just one.

I feel like with the US I get a bigger life, I feel freer to pioneer, to be an entrepreneur. I feel that in some ways there is greater social mobility. England felt strangely class-bound when I was there and I like the chance to reach beyond that sort of thing. I remember when I first landed here I noticed that so many of the women's mags had articles/stories on starting your own business. I don't remember seeing that in the UK.

There's a lot I still wrestle with; I find the political landscape unnecessarily polarizing; the US needs a third party! I cannot make sense of the fears about healthcare – it seems a no-brainer to me, the current system is insane. I find the way we file taxes annually weirdly antiquated. The news is entertainment and I keep wondering why the female news readers wear full makeup and cocktail dresses. The racial dynamics are depressing and debilitating – a permanent rumbling volcano.

And yet I love living here. My children were born here so my roots are now here. And yet, whenever I go to London and I walk through the city I am incredibly emotional. I feel a huge amount of love for London at a visceral level. I go to the National and I stand and stare at Constable paintings and it triggers memories of me as a 17-year-old dreaming of a life I was determined to fight for. I look at Big Ben, I walk along the Embankment – it's like some kind of urban pilgrimage! London is under my skin. I think it always will be.

But America is my home – not my country yet – but my home. And I've felt called here since I was 14, so even in the strange in-between two worlds we sometimes feel – I know I'm meant to feel it on this side of the Atlantic.

**Amy:** Would you be slimmer? I don't know. We had an American over for dinner last week and he said how the food here in the UK is so heavy (but not what I served him). I asked where he had been eating, and he said pubs. Well of course!

But I love that I walk so much here – the school runs and popping out to Tesco and avoiding the car if I can. America just isn't made for walking like London life is – I'd never dream of driving into London, but for you to go to Minneapolis or St Paul you have to. My dad took the bus to work in Minneapolis every day, but I think he was an exception and not the rule.

The class system gets me too. Doesn't seem to trouble my hubby so much; he seems to accept it. Working class, middle class, UMC, blah blah blah. I pretend I don't fit in to any of the classes, being the outsider, when someone tries to slot me somewhere class-wise or as a VW (vicar's wife). But you touch on racial issues, which I know can be huge in America as we hear about Ferguson and all the connected pain – I wonder if race is more the shaping issue for Americans to grapple with, while issues of social mobility are those Brits should address. I think the way class hits me relates to confidence – I feel "edited" sometimes when I try to be myself in Britain, like I hit a wall of disapproval ("We don't do things like that in this country"). It's easy for me to shrink back and give up too quickly.

But the NHS – I'm totally with you there; it's an imperfect treasure. I grill my US friends and family, asking them how much they pay in healthcare, and I'm astounded. Parents put off taking their kids to the doctor because it'll incur deductibles, and people don't even call an ambulance when they are having a heart attack because of the financial implications. In the UK we don't think twice about going to the GP and I shudder to think of all the dosh we'd have to pay for Joshua on healthcare if we were Stateside. But I sometimes fear about getting cancer in the UK – would the treatments be quick and effective? And the waiting times can be hard. What gets me most, however, is how much we have to push as advocates to release the medical care. It's easy for me to do so on behalf of my kids, but less so for myself. Maybe that's true in either country, but it feels like we have to win over the doctors here because healthcare is a limited resource.

But you're right; where we're living comes down to God's call. Whether our home is in the States or Britain or some other nation, we live as strangers and foreigners and that makes us remember the country we'll welcome as our own . . .

Swapping lives, with the chance to see the pressures and joys on either side of the Pond, made me even more thankful for this one-toe-on-each-side-of-the-Atlantic life, for a heart that beats for each country and its people. I knew our house swap was a gift with layers of meaning to keep unwrapping. For instance, when I might become tempted to think that "All would be better over there," I could remember passive-aggressive behaviour or the ever-present need for a car or the passion of churchgoers in the UK. I had seen some of the joys and challenges in both countries, realizing anew that neither system is perfect and both have their weakness and strengths.

The house-swap experience reminded me that life is a journey, and that God can burst our expectations – such as how meeting someone like Nicholas has led me to a wildly different set of life experiences than I would have ever dreamed possible, or for Jo and Chris, how their travelling to the States so many years ago has led them to their nomadic but missional and settled existence now as they raise two American daughters. For each of us, the key is to be present where we are, and to be present with God, even though we have bits of our hearts lodged in different places in the world. We may think that we are losing ourselves – our heritage and ways of life – but we see that through the sacrifices we actually find ourselves. As I said to Jo, I might feel "edited" here in Britain, but I have received gifts from the process as well. Just as I've seen my text in this book smoothed out and made more readable, with pet phrases and anecdotes removed that may have been stumbling blocks to readers, so too I can see how the rough and tumble of feeling awkward in a foreign land can result in a less angular, more polished person. For this life-editing means I wrestle with who I am before God, and I consider how much of my resistance to being shaped comes from a different culture and how much from a sinful nature or my personality. As I view the slimmed down version of the book, I ask for eyes to see the slimmed down version of my life.

And like Jo with her calling to the States, I know that for such a time as this I'm called to this island, this place, this people. And that's enough.

As I write, Jessica enjoys her last playdate with a British-Nigerian-American friend who in a fortnight will move to America. Jessica has many plans for us to travel to see her friend in the summer, even though I try to explain how Minnesota where we visit and Virginia where her friend's new home will be are separated by a thousand miles. My daughter will learn the pain of separation, but I hope, too, the gift of friendship that spans geography. I wish I could cushion her from the ache she will feel in days to come, but if I can point her to the Source of hope, love, and life, I know that I will have been a good mother. And that too will be enough.

# EPILOGUE: LIQUID LOVE

When I had been living in the UK for eight months, we moved to Surrey to Nicholas's first curacy, but our house wasn't yet available. Feeling down, I wrote in my journal:

> At times it seems so hard being a foreigner. Reading my Psalm for the day brought such thoughts to my mind. The Psalmist is crying out: "Reach down your hand from on high; deliver me and rescue me from the mighty waters, from the hands of foreigners whose mouths are full of lies, whose right hands are deceitful" (Psalm 144:7–8). Some of these here in England will have mouths full of lies and right hands that are deceitful.
>
> Being a foreigner makes me feel always a little bit different; I don't ever fully fit in. There are times when the differences can be melted away and one doesn't feel quite so jarred, as when with a kindred spirit woman friend.
>
> Coming "home" to England after two weeks in France was odd. It was nice to be able to hear English, but it didn't feel like home. Surely if we had actually had a home to come to, and not temporary accommodation, it would have felt different. Still, it was nice to come to roses by the bedside and freshly laundered sheets, and a meal on the table.

I identified as a foreigner and a stranger; this is how I must have projected my identity to those around me. I was fearful of the mouths of others, which I thought would wound and pierce.

Over the years I've journeyed from seeing myself as a stranger to a friend as I've found myself in Britain, realizing that my stance of being a foreigner was rooted in fear, not love. When I started to peel back the layers of self-consciousness, breaking through the barriers of accent, class, or preconceptions, I began to see these so-called "foreign people" instead as individuals with hearts that love, hands that serve, and words that affirm. People to love; people to love me. Instead of taking a defensive stance, anticipating rejection, I can lower the dividing walls and welcome a conversation. I can hope to move past stereo-types and expectations to understanding and communion.

Such as what happened one day on a train from Coventry to London. Many times on such a journey I prefer to keep to myself, introverted preferences winning out over breaking social convention and chatting with my neighbour. I had been in Coventry speaking on the adventures of prayer, and the day had been a special one of us sensing God's presence and love. Maybe I was buoyed up by how he had revealed himself to us in the sessions.

I couldn't help but overhear the young woman next to me on her mobile as we approached London. She was going to Marylebone, but didn't know how to pronounce it, nervous-ness radiating from her.

When she hung up, I said, "Mar-lee-bone – is that where you're going?"

Surprised that I would initiate a conversation, she said, "Oh, is that how you pronounce it?"

We chatted and I reassured her about where she was heading, and how to get there on the Tube from Euston Station, where our train was terminating. I don't remember how the conversation became so deep so quickly, but she shared that her mother had died recently, and although she had tried to reach her through a séance, she had also gone to a church, seeking peace. I tried to gently warn her against the stuff of the occult, and she said that actually she had been thoroughly creeped out by the experience. We chatted about church and God, and amazingly, her name was Amy, so I told her mine was too, and did she know the meaning was "beloved"? I said I would pray for her, certainly remembering her name.

After bidding her farewell, I marvelled at the encounter and the depth of our sharing. I prayed as I travelled home on the Tube for this Amy, that she would find comfort and meaning through the true and living God.

The greatest longing and ache of living in the UK is the separation from my family and friends. When I left, my niece was four and my nephew was two; now they are adults and I've missed much of their formative years. My parents are active and healthy, but I realized recently with a jolt that they won't be around forever. When I'm missing them I'll pick up the phone (if it's not their middle of the night) or send them a line; sometimes I remind myself that we'll have eternity together when God himself will dwell with us.

Though I ache at times, living here has brought me an abundance of blessings. Some include cultural and historical delights, such as a tour of the Houses of Parliament with our MP or taking in the beauty of the Farne Islands or the famous Gold Hill in Dorset. I can better understand British authors such as Shakespeare, Jane Austen, Thomas Hardy, and CS Lewis, having been immersed in the culture and visited their haunts. I have a new appreciation for the monarchy through Joshua, and through listening to Nicholas name all the monarchs and their dates of birth and death. I have an instant connection with others who live as expats. And I have left behind a trail of power showers for other clergy families, although I haven't always been able to introduce mixer taps.

Yet the deeper blessings are the changes that living here has wrought in me. My borders have been enlarged, and I now know and care more about more of the world through visiting different countries and meeting people from many nations. I also understand more about my country of birth, having seen it through the eyes of others. I love the diversity that living in a big city brings. Last week, for instance, I shared an evening with my community book club and revelled in the links to Japan, Serbia, India, South Africa, and Australia.

And supremely, my confidence is strengthened as I ask God for an eternal perspective. Pondering the Psalms, and especially those of David, informs and encourages me, such as Psalm 16:5–6: "LORD, you alone are my portion and my cup; you make my lot secure. The boundary lines have fallen for me in pleasant places; surely I have a delightful inheritance."

Sometimes these boundary lines feel constraining – we yearn for unfettered freedom. But we don't have God's perspective; we don't realize that if we escape the fences, leaving our verdant green patch, we'll be out in the wilderness, subject to bulls, foxes, and other vermin. The boundary lines give us a place to flourish; a place to call home; a place to find ourselves.

And when I realize that the *Lord* has drawn my boundary lines, my attitude shifts. After all, he has called me here to this place and to these people. He gives me security – my grounding and my foundation; he bequeaths on me an inheritance – my vision and heavenly perspective. He has brought me to this pleasant place.

And with King David, I say:

Lord, you're my portion
You're my cup
You make my lot secure.

And these boundary lines?
They're in pleasant places
Delightful, my inheritance.

I'm content.
I'm grateful.
I'm yours.

When Nicholas and I planned our wedding, we wanted the sermon to focus on John 12, the story of Jesus at dinner with his friends in Bethany. The writing in the gospel is sparse: Martha served. Lazarus – back from the dead – reclined at the table with Jesus. Mary poured out pure nard. Captured by the idea of extravagant giving, we hoped it would characterize our marriage.

As I think about this passage, I ponder on each of the friends with Jesus. There's Lazarus, reclining. Was it an act of extravagance for him to return from the dead? Having seen the wonders of heaven, he may not have wanted to come back to the dusty earth, a place of disease, hurt, and pain.

And there's Martha, serving again. Was she happy to serve? Did she feel safe in the role? Was she pouring herself out in extravagant service, just as Mary was pouring out the expensive nard? We don't know. But I have met many people who have a magnificent gift of service. They are often quiet and humble and may stay in the background, but they are the ones putting chairs away or serving the coffee or doing other behind-the-scenes work. When I marvel at their efforts, they smile quietly, without fuss.

In terms of Martha, I like to think that her attitude had changed from the first time we see Jesus meeting this family,[1] when she was distraught that Mary wasn't pulling her weight with all the preparations. Then Jesus said that she had got things wrong, and that Mary was doing the right thing by sitting at his feet. In this story Martha is still serving, but maybe now she's doing it out of love and devotion, not mere duty.

And Mary, the giver of gifts, breaks open the expensive nard and anoints Jesus' feet with her hair. She is criticized for her sacrifice, but Jesus sees her heart and knows that her act of devotion will be a legacy of love. She doesn't care what the others think of her – if they see her as a loose woman or wasteful. She pours out love in liquid form.

Not only back then, but today Jesus asks us to break our expensive nard. I didn't realize the deep cost of pouring out this precious liquid in marrying Nicholas as I left behind family, friends, and the way of life I knew. At first it was a great adventure, moving abroad and finding out about a different culture and way of life. But then the sheen wore off and eventually children came along, with the resulting pull of grandparents and family becoming even stronger. Can I continue to give willingly and extravagantly?

Most would see pouring out that expensive perfume as costly; some even as a waste. I feel the sacrifice of investing our lives in the UK, depriving my parents of their grandchildren and being separated every Christmas and Easter. Of the birthdays and anniversaries that pass with gifts and cards purchased ahead of time to avoid expensive postage, but no face time together. Of the health crises that come and go and we aren't there to support each other. Yet I have to believe that pouring out the costly nard is worth the sacrifice, or I would move tomorrow.

Sometimes the feelings of disconnect pop up, for I miss my family, and in one sense I'm not "settled," as an older friend asks me. By the nature of our marriage one of us will always be away from our country of birth (and of course by living in the UK we are near Nicholas's parents, with the benefits that entails). Any disconnect reminds us that we are pilgrims and strangers in this land, and that our true citizenship is to be heavenly citizens here on earth. For in that place, we'll have the biggest reunion party ever. No more tears; no more pain; no more longing; no more separated family members. And the fragrance of the pure nard will fill our senses.

Extravagant giving to one looks different than the extravagant giving of another. For one person, it might be opening their heart to a new person, or opening their heart to God a crack wider. He doesn't force open our hearts, but floods the slivers we offer with his light and love. At first we may clutch at the door, but with God's love and grace we can fling it open as his light shines in and transforms our world.

In thankfulness we give back to him, for we receive his love from a place of safety. After all, when we know we are loved, we can love. When we find ourselves, we can share with others. When our house is built on solid foundations, we can open the doors and let people in. When we receive the gifts of

God, we can shed an outlook of scarcity – we don't need to be stingy, for we know there will be enough.

We love an extravagant God who holds nothing back. He will not restrict the floodgates of his love, for if his people would open their hearts and their lives, he will come in. With his love he imparts to us love for others – even those whom we may think are unloveable. He can transform even the hard relationships in our lives – our spouses or children or in-laws or neighbours or friends. His liquid love will repair the relationships and bring hope. His liquid love brings belonging and meaning and peace and radiance. His liquid love brings the sweet smell that fills the home, for all who enter will smell it and feel it and experience it. His liquid love is freely given, for he pours himself out for his people.

He says come:

Come
All who thirst
Come
All without money
Come
Buy wine and eat
Come
Without money or cost
Come.

Listen to me
Come
Eat what is good
Come
Delight in the richest of fare

Come
Give ear and listen
Come
My promises to you forever
Come.

And as the rain and snow
Fall from heaven,
Watering the earth,
Making it bud and flourish,
Yielding seed for sower
And bread for the eater . . .
So will my word accomplish my desires.
It will not return to me empty,
But will achieve my purposes and plans.

So go out in joy!
Be led forth in peace!
Burst into song
With the mountains and hills;
Clap your hands
With the trees of the field.
For instead of the thornbush
The juniper grows.
Instead of briars
We see myrtle.

And this –
Yes this,
Is for the everlasting renown
Of the Lord.[2]

# AFTERWORD

## LOOKING BACK AND AHEAD WITH GRATITUDE AND HOPE

Starting this ten-year anniversary afterword on our twenty-seventh wedding anniversary feels fitting and yet poignant. After all, I never planned to make my home on this island for nearly three decades – our agreement, when Nicholas and I married, was that we'd live here for five to seven years and then move to my native land, where Nicholas's accent would be the noticeable one. But that's not been our experience, nor God's call.

As I recount in chapter 20, I sensed God inviting me to give up my campaign to return to the States when our kids were newly in primary school.[1] I don't think I've heard God's voice more clearly before or since, and wrestling with this gentle but firm invitation felt intense, challenging, and then freeing. As I pondered and prayed, I realized that my desire to move was keeping me from embracing life here. On a minor level, I didn't want to buy new bookshelves or expensive electrical items that wouldn't travel with us; more deeply, my reticence meant I closed off my heart to interactions and friendships, adventures, and ways to serve. With a lot of inner struggle, and after arranging our books on their new shelves, I released the idea of moving. As the weeks, months, and years passed, I've been surprised and enriched by God's gifts as he's embedded our family here.

As I think about finding myself in Britain, I see how I continue to find myself in Christ, within my family, in my service and work, and indeed in Britain. And I notice how God keeps his promises. He's surprised me with experiences that I wouldn't have dreamed possible even a decade ago when this, my first book, was published. In my professional life, for instance, I've pursued a master's degree in Christian spirituality, I've written six more books/resources, and I've moved fully into spiritual direction, accompanying people in their life with God. I find joy in leading retreats in the UK and Spain, revelling in "thin spaces" with God on the windswept shores of the island of Iona or in the stark beauty of the Valley of the Rocks in Devon. But even more than the amazing splendour of the landscape are the wonderful people I've met – their welcome, friendship, and affection. Although I don't think that I'll ever fully understand their banter and humour.

I give thanks for God's grace and abundance in my years here in the UK but I know that relinquishing my dream of living in the States entails its own cost. I think about missing my parents' significant wedding anniversaries, the birth of my grand-niece (even though my daughter and I flew from Minnesota to New York that very day), and not sharing the many celebrations of birthdays, Thanksgiving, Christmas, and other special days. The high days and holidays stand out in my mind, but I'm aware too of not being present for the everyday lunches, the times of "just popping over" to a friend or family member's home, the enjoying of games and gatherings.

And yet, and yet. Amazingly, God connects us over the miles, and today's technological improvements help so much. Time zones may separate us, as my weary body reminds me when I get up in the middle of the night to watch an American football game, but the ease of video chats and text messages has increased my relating to loved ones, friends, colleagues, and readers far away. I love the deep connections I enjoy with kindred spirits through these recent advances – my closest friends, I realize, are those I only rarely see in person.

In all of the experiences, those good and hard, I trust that God cares for us and provides in ways we couldn't engineer, and I call to mind his promises that he'll be with us always. He'll not abandon us when we miss those dear to us, when we face scary diagnoses, when we endure the pain of heartaches, when we ache with the sadness of disappointment. He showers us with love and he welcomes us to embrace joy, even in times of tears, as he comforts us and gives us hope. Through his Spirit living within us he bridges the gaps, such as when he prompts a friend to contact me just when I need it most or when a loved one comes for a visit. (Especially if they come bearing Ranch dressing or Everything bagel seasoning.) God really does meet all of our needs.

Ten years on, my journey of finding myself continues. Perhaps that will always be the case, as throughout my life I find myself in God, in Christ, through the work of the Holy Spirit. As I come to know God more fully I am more fully known – including to myself.

I didn't realize a decade ago that launching my first book into the world would help me in this journey of becoming more of who God has created me to be, but it did. It paved the way for me to own my voice, to speak forth my beliefs and views, to share my love for and understanding of God. As I reread the text now, I notice with gratitude the sprinklings of my passion for encountering God through prayer, which in the past decade have been my main focus in my writing and speaking.

An important part of that journey was my brief foray into the world of academia for a master's degree in Christian spirituality. I longed to feast from the riches of the saints of old but my heart pounded with nerves when I first walked along the hallowed halls of a Jesuit college in the University of London. I loved "meeting" and making friends with some of these amazing Christians – such as Teresa of Avila and Julian of Norwich – but I found the rigours of an English postgraduate degree surprising. The cut and thrust of the debate of ideas was not something I was used to, and often I felt lacking. I kept on with my reading and essays with sometimes exhausted determination, and with the encouragement of family and friends.

Looking back over that time, I understand now that I didn't experience a flash of insight that propelled me forward in thinking deeply, but rather God's long, slow work led me to drink from his wells of wisdom and insight. As I gained confidence in my ability to think and explore different ideas, I found myself growing more into who God had made me to be. And when I received a distinction on my dissertation, I verily whooped in celebration![2]

How about you? Perhaps as you look back over your life, you too will grasp how God has been changing you bit by bit, day by day. So often we understand his grace in reverse as we grasp how God is making us more like Jesus – more wise, caring, thoughtful, kind, patient. Whereas in the moments of frustration or overwhelm, we fear that the challenges of relationships, projects, failed dreams, or something else will topple us and we won't have the needed strength or courage to do the next thing. Bravery often looks like imaginatively grabbing the hand of Jesus and getting out of bed to go to school, work, or church where we face deadlines, hard tasks, and perhaps conflict of some kind.

I invite you to take some time to consider a period of your life, asking God to help you see it from his point of view. He may reveal to you his slow but sure work, how he's been changing and transforming you. As part of this you could prayerfully receive a blessing that highlights God's maturing process. Below is a sort of prayer that you could read slowly and thoughtfully, asking God:

- to increase your ability to persevere if you yearn for your struggles to be behind you;
- for a flash of insight of how God sees you and your life – your concerns, hopes, dreams, fears;
- for a deepening of your trust that God will follow through on his promises to love you, to never leave you, to remain actively concerned about you and those whom you love.

Here is "Patient Trust" by Pierre Teilhard de Chardin, a French Jesuit priest and scientist from the turn of the twentieth century:

Above all, trust in the slow work of God.
We are quite naturally impatient in everything to reach the end without delay.

We should like to skip the intermediate stages.
We are impatient of being on the way to something unknown,
  something new.

And yet it is the law of all progress
that it is made by passing through some stages of instability –
and that it may take a very long time.

And so I think it is with you;
your ideas mature gradually – let them grow,
let them shape themselves, without undue haste.
Don't try to force them on,
as though you could be today what time
(that is to say, grace and circumstances acting on your own
  good will)
will make of you tomorrow.

Only God could say what this new spirit
gradually forming within you will be.
Give Our Lord the benefit of believing
that his hand is leading you,
and accept the anxiety of feeling yourself
in suspense and incomplete.[3]

My family has grown and developed in the ten years since this book was released, with our kids now nearly and newly adults – this year our son finishes university and our daughter film school. Witnessing the people they are and are becoming, with their particular passions and gifts, brings us joy and hope.

In the past decade, like other families, we've had our ups and downs. As I've recounted elsewhere, Nicholas faced a time of deep mental distress after his mother died, which set off some family conflicts and other issues. As a result he experienced anxiety and depression, including being signed off from work.[4] Then during the pandemic, our kids like others experienced the major shift of having to stay home, missing out on interaction with friends and peers as we all shielded and school went online. As we navigated those stormy waters, God was faithful, although I sometimes wondered how he kept the crashing waves from sinking us. But they didn't. We may bear some scars from the heartache and pain, but I trust we've become more resilient.

I have to admit that I've found it challenging to write this afterword as I've resisted returning in my memory to the decade's hard and sometimes excruciating experiences. Yet I recognize that I'm not alone in facing unwanted trials. Behind the statistics for increased mental struggles and illnesses are beloved individuals and their families and friends, each seeking glimmers of light through the seeming all-encompassing fog. As I witness people experiencing these agonies, my heart hurts and I turn to God, begging for his mercy and release. I trust in our faithful God, but I also wish life didn't have to be so hard.

Looking to a bigger scale, I note that these last ten years have been a time of collective stress. Consider, for instance, the increased number of natural disasters, with floods, fires, earthquakes, and hurricanes wreaking havoc and displacing many from their homes. People seem more divided now too, with the shouting across the aisles feeling more commonplace than a shared desire to seek the common good. The cost of living has increased, affecting the downtrodden and weary, adding angst and fear. At times it can all feel just too much.

For me, walking through the valley has often felt like trudging at a snail's pace, placing one muddy foot in front of the other with my gaze turned downward. At times I might feel like I'm falling, but the pit hasn't swallowed me up. I feel the arms of those supporting us in prayer upholding us, and of course the everlasting arms of God underneath me.[5]

Praying along with Psalm 23 helps me to look up, and it brings immediate comfort and strengthens my faith.[6] Simply take this most beloved Psalm and personalize it – tell God how you need him, in this moment, to meet your needs. Thus you could say that the Lord is my Comforter, Healer, Guide, Friend, Provider, and so on. Putting ourselves with our current situations into the words of David helps us to receive God's love and words of consolation. This way of praying can help us to move from our heads to our hearts.

If you're currently mired in the valley of the shadow of death, I pray that God, the Good Shepherd, would give you comfort, hope, strength, and protection.

This year, a big change for our family will be moving to a new church and community. As I recount in the introduction, in the early years of our marriage we moved four times in five years, but then we stayed over two decades in north London, establishing ourselves in this community and giving our kids stability as they grew up. Now there's a whiff of coming home as we move to southwest London, to a stone's throw from Nicholas's first curacy in Surrey, where we had our first home together.

But the journey to our new home means leaving familiar surroundings and decades-long relationships, such as those with members of my book club or friends at the gym. For our kids, moving from their childhood home entails a different sort of loss – leaving their oldest of friends, their memories of school days and playgrounds, and their lovely Victorian home, with its gracious high ceilings and atmospheric fireplaces.

Even considering the word *uprooting* brings to mind a plant with roots deprived of the rich soil they'd formerly burrowed into. Our family might experience some of the shock of being placed into new soil – the wilting of our leaves, the seeming lack of growth. Thus in this time of being transplanted I'm clinging to the promised mercies of God and our sense of his leading and guiding.

For instance, on a retreat day a few months ago, I found encouragement as I shared with a lovely French woman some of my fears about settling into a new place. She said how God had led her to Acts 17:26 when she and her family felt called to the UK: "From one man [God] made all the nations, that they should inhabit the whole earth; and he marked out their appointed times in history and the boundaries of their lands." Leaning into those words, I've been considering that if God marks out this new space for us in southwest London – these new boundaries of land (which fits in nicely with the parish system in the Church of England[7]) – then I can trust he'll lead us to spaciousness and growth. I hope that in these pastures new we will love and serve, and from there our kids will launch fully into their adult lives. Even if the uprooting feels a wrench.

Leaving this beloved place in north London has led me to ponder again the notion of home. I'm reminded that God's story in the Bible engages with this theme from the beginning to the end – we see our first parents being uprooted from their home in the Garden of Eden in Genesis and we witness God's people finding that ultimate city of home, with its healing tree by the life-giving river, in Revelation. Throughout its pages, God is our Homemaker who calls us to make our home with him.

How do you find your sense of home? A way to think about this prayerfully is to engage your imagination, asking God to show you how he is the architect and creator of your house: "For every house is built by someone, but God is the builder of everything."[8] You might find yourself walking, through your imaginings, along various rooms in a familiar house, such as your childhood home, or you might explore a wholly new structure, something that expresses who you are. Perhaps reading the words of CS Lewis, where he plays with a parable by George MacDonald, helps as you engage imaginatively:

> Imagine yourself as a living house. God comes in to rebuild that house. At first, perhaps, you can understand what He is doing. He is getting the drains right and stopping the leaks in the roof and so on: you knew that those jobs needed doing and so you are not surprised. But presently he starts knocking the house about in a way that hurts abominably and does not seem to make sense. What on earth is He up to? The explanation is that He is building quite a different house from the one you thought of – throwing out a new wing here, putting on an extra floor there, running up towers, making courtyards. You thought you were going to be made into a decent little cottage: but He is building a palace. He intends to come and live in it Himself.[9]

As we bring this journey to a close, I want to thank you, friend, for joining with me. As I bid you farewell for now, I pray that you'll receive the enfolding love of God throughout the seasons of your life.

May you experience, in your goings-out and comings-home:
    the joy of adventure,
    the wonder of return,
    the inspiration of the Spirit.

May you know:
    the warmth of the Creator,
    the friendship of the Saviour,
    the advocacy of the Spirit.

May you find yourself in God:
    your deepest longings,
    your truest self,
    your place of belonging,
    your home.

# RECIPES

I suppose I shouldn't be surprised that Americans and British measure, bake, and cook differently. When I first moved to the UK, a visiting American friend and I were eating at a pub, and when he asked what a courgette was, I hesitated before saying, "It's green and a bit like a cucumber." Only later when I was at a big supermarket (grocery store), and I spotted a list of vegetables with their various names in the produce section, did I realize a courgette is just a zucchini.

Americans favour the cup/tablespoon way of baking, although cooks who prefer a precise standard of measuring are starting to use the European system of weighing the ingredients out. I'm more of an intuitive cook and usually get it right, but sometimes when I rely on my memory I make a mess of things.

I've tried to cater for both sides of the Pond by including American and British names and measurements in the recipes. A few particulars: I haven't distinguished between granulated and caster/superfine sugar, as the default for US recipes tends to be granulated. Also, baking powder in the recipes refers to that found in the States. In the UK you can substitute ¼ teaspoon of the baking powder found here plus ½ teaspoon cream of tartar for every teaspoon of US baking powder.

I've adapted the recipes from various sources – the Wiese family cookbook as compiled by my mom's second cousin Carolyn Darlington (also married to a Brit!), my mom's recipe box, cookbooks and magazines. Because I've been away from my family-of-origin for so many years, I've had to learn to make the family recipes myself or forsake the traditions. I've relied heavily on my mom's advice over the phone as she's given me tips on how to make the various dishes and baking delights. I've tried to capture her hints here for you; I hope all will be clear and you'll enjoy these memory-making foods from our kitchen to yours.

# THANKSGIVING FEAST

Thanksgiving in the States brings together people as the country stops to feast, watch American football, and feast some more. Roast turkey is the main event, accompanied by mashed potatoes, sweet potatoes, stuffing, gravy, and vegetables. Which side dishes appear varies by region, as well as which desserts – but most people would agree on pumpkin or apple pie.

## *Stuffing*

In my experience, American stuffing differs from the British sort; I find the latter dry and unappealing, compared with the crispy-on-the-outside, sticky-on-the-inside variety I'm used to. Making stuffing is an art, not a science, so don't be afraid to experiment with the amounts of bread, onion, and celery. I usually make a huge batch – double the quantity below. I always make the Minnesota wild rice for Thanksgiving, so I chop the onions and celery for both recipes and sauté them together before dividing out the portions for the stuffing and rice dishes. In terms of seasoning the stuffing, I play around with how much of the various herbs and spices I include, tasting my way to stuffing perfection.

# STUFFING

## Ingredients

- 1 loaf of bread, crusts removed if you prefer, cut in cubes and left to dry a day ahead, or crisped up under the grill
- 1 medium-large onion, chopped
- 3 sticks celery, chopped
- 1 cup (about 100 g) dried cranberries (or less, according to preference)
- 2 teaspoons salt
- 2 teaspoons black pepper
- 2 tablespoons dried parsley, or ¼ cup (5 g) chopped fresh parsley
- ¾ teaspoon ground thyme, or 1½ teaspoons thyme leaves, crushed
- ¾ teaspoon ground sage, or 1½ teaspoons sage leaves, crushed
- (Can also add ½ teaspoon paprika, and/or ¾ teaspoon rosemary, and/or ½ teaspoon tarragon)
- Turkey or chicken stock to moisten – about 2 cups (400 ml)

## Directions

1. Sauté the onions and celery together in a couple of tablespoons of olive oil until soft.

2. Add mixture to the bread cubes, and then stir in the cranberries and seasoning.

3. Add some stock to moisten the mixture, little by little, until you reach the right consistency. The mixture should feel moist, not mushy.

4. Press into a lightly greased 13 x 9 in (33 x 23 cm) pan (baking tin or Pyrex dish) and bake in a 350°F/180°C/gas mark 4 oven for 45 minutes to an hour, until the top is brown and crunchy. You can also use some of the mixture to stuff the neck of your bird (most food hygiene experts now agree it's safest not to stuff the cavity).

*Serves 10.*

# SWEET POTATOES

## Ingredients

- 7–8 sweet potatoes
- ¼ cup (50 g) butter
- ¼ cup (50 g) light brown sugar
- 1 cup (190 g) dried apricots, cut into small pieces

## Directions

1. Peel the potatoes and cut into large chunks. Boil in a saucepan with water until soft – about 30 minutes – then drain, saving some of the cooking water.

2. Mash the potatoes and then stir in the butter and brown sugar, adding a little of the reserved liquid if needed to reach the desired consistency.

3. Add the dried apricots, put it all into an oven-proof dish, and cover with foil.

4. Bake in a 325°F/165°C/gas mark 3 oven for about 30 minutes.

   *Serves 10.*

## Minnesota Wild Rice

To me, Thanksgiving wouldn't be Thanksgiving without Minnesota wild rice. It's not actually a rice, but a cereal grain that grows in the many fresh, cool lakes in northern Minnesota. For centuries, the native peoples in Minnesota have harvested this grain by hand, travelling throughout the lakes by canoe. Look for it in large supermarkets in the UK or health-food stores, but for this recipe avoid buying the packets combined with white rice.

# MINNESOTA WILD RICE

## Ingredients

- 2½ cups (450 g) wild rice
- 4 cups (1 litre) stock, either beef, poultry, or vegetarian
- 3 sticks celery, sliced
- 1 onion, chopped
- 2 cups (225 g) chestnut mushrooms, thickly sliced
- Olive oil

## Directions

1. Soak the rice for an hour in cold water, then rinse and drain.

2. Sauté the celery and onion in a large pan with the olive oil until soft, then add the rice and stock.

3. Bring to the boil and simmer for 45 minutes to an hour, until the rice is tender and most of the liquid is absorbed.

4. Add the mushrooms and cook at a higher heat for the last 5 minutes, until all of the liquid has evaporated.

*Serves 10.*

# FROSTY PUMPKIN PIE

## Ingredients

- 9 in (23 cm) pie crust, baked, or (my preference) a 300 g package of ginger cookies (biscuits) crushed and combined with a knob of melted butter (2 to 3 tablespoons), pressed into your pie dish and frozen
- 1 cup pumpkin puree (I use a standard-size 425 g can, which can now easily be found in the UK at large supermarkets or online)
- ½ cup packed (100 g) light brown sugar
- ½ teaspoon salt
- ½ teaspoon cinnamon
- ½ teaspoon ginger
- ¼ teaspoon nutmeg
- 4 cups vanilla ice cream, softened (I use about two-thirds of a 2 litre tub of soft-scoop ice cream)

## Directions

1. Beat together the pumpkin, brown sugar, salt, and spices. Fold in the ice cream.

2. Pour the pumpkin and ice cream mixture into the prepared pie shell. Freeze until firm.

3. Remove from the freezer 20–30 minutes before serving, so it's slightly softened and easier to cut. Garnish with whipped cream and, if you like, walnut halves.

*Serves 8–10.*

# A VW After-Church Buffet

One after-church buffet that stands out in my mind was the first event held in our new church centre for the lunch after Jessica's baptism. It was February and the builders hadn't yet sorted out the issues with the heating, so we ate with our coats and gloves on. I made a range of salads, which were tasty but cold! Here are some interesting ones to add to a selection of rolls, cold meats and, if you must, quiches.

## BROCCOLI BACON SALAD

### Ingredients

- 4 cups broccoli florets (about 1–2 bunches)
- 6 slices streaky bacon
- ½ cup (70 g) sunflower seeds (or ½ cup [35 g] of sliced almonds, toasted)
- 1 cup (175 g) red seedless grapes, halved
- 1 cup (175 g) green seedless grapes, halved
- 1 red onion, chopped (or 3 stalks of green [spring] onions)
- 1 cup (240 g) low-fat mayonnaise
- ¼ cup (50 g) sugar
- 2 tablespoons vinegar

### Directions

1. Fry the bacon until crispy. Drain, and remove the excess fat by patting dry with paper towel (kitchen roll); chop or crumble into small pieces.

2. In a large bowl, combine the broccoli, bacon, sunflower seeds or almonds, grapes, and onion.

3. In another bowl, combine mayonnaise, sugar, and vinegar. Add to the broccoli mixture and stir to coat.

4. Chill at least 4 hours, or overnight, to combine the flavours.

*Serves 8.*

# SWEET POTATO & GREEN BEAN SALAD

## Ingredients

- 3–4 stalks green (spring) onions, chopped
- ½ cup (160 g) mango chutney
- 3 tablespoons olive oil
- 2 tablespoons cider vinegar
- ½ teaspoon salt
- Freshly ground black pepper
- 6 cups (about 1.5 kg) sweet potato, peeled and chopped into small cubes
- 2 cups (about 0.5 kg) green (French) beans, trimmed and cut in half
- 3–4 tablespoons chopped fresh cilantro (coriander)

## Directions

1. Combine the onions, chutney, oil, vinegar, salt and pepper.

2. Cook the potatoes in a saucepan with water, bringing to the boil and simmering for 15 minutes or until just tender; drain and let cool while you cook the beans.

3. Cook the beans in boiling salted water for 4 minutes until tender but still crisp. Drain and rinse beneath cold water.

4. Combine potatoes, beans, and cilantro (coriander), and add the chutney dressing, tossing to coat. Serve slightly warm or at room temperature.

*Serves 8.*

# CABBAGE SLAW WITH POPPY-SEED DRESSING

## Ingredients

- 4 tablespoons cider vinegar
- 1 tablespoon runny honey
- 1 tablespoon Dijon mustard
- 1 tablespoon chopped fresh dill
- 2 teaspoons poppy seeds
- 2 teaspoons olive oil
- Salt and pepper to taste
- 2 cups (200 g) thinly sliced green cabbage
- 2 cups (200 g) thinly sliced red cabbage
- 1 cup (90 g) carrots, cut into sticks (or grated with a food processor)

## Directions

1. Combine the vinegar, honey, mustard, dill, poppy seeds, oil, salt and pepper.

2. Add the cabbage and carrots and toss to coat.

   *Serves 8.*

# CHRISTMAS EVE FEAST

## *The Wiese Family Chicken Noodle Soup*

### *Noodles*

Early in the day, make the noodles. Beat 6–8 eggs, adding a dash of salt. Add flour (all-purpose [plain] flour) in stages, mixing it thoroughly and adding enough so that you can form 2 or 3 soft balls. Spread a little flour on your rolling pin and the surface where you will roll out the noodles. Roll out each of the dough balls into thin – as thin as you can – circles, flipping the dough over when it gets sticky and sprinkling more flour on top as needed.

Set out the dough circles to dry for 3–4 hours. Take care not to leave them out overnight, or they will become too dry. Flip them over halfway through to ensure even drying. Once dry (the edges will curl slightly), roll several sheets up together loosely. Now cut the noodles, slicing them as thinly as you can without breaking them. Separate the noodles and set aside – you could lay them out flat, but I usually just fluff them to keep them from sticking together in a big mound. (You can also freeze them at this point for later use.)

### *Chicken*

Add a whole chicken to a large stockpot filled with cold water. To make the stock richer, add a couple of carrots, an onion or leek, and some peppercorns (and any old veg you may have hanging around in your fridge). Bring the water to the boil and reduce the heat. Cook for about an hour (uncovered), until the chicken is tender. Remove the chicken from the stock and, once it's fairly cool, remove the meat from the bones, cut or tear into chunks, and set aside. (Yes, your hands will get greasy but think of it as a good moisturizing session.) Return the bones and skin to the stock and gently boil, uncovered, for another couple of hours.

About an hour or so before you will eat, remove the bones and veg from the stock, taking care not to throw the stock down the drain! Skim away any fat from the stock and add a chopped-up onion and carrots (and celery if you like). Let it cook for a while and then add your noodles, stirring them so that they don't stick together. Add your chicken and season with a bit of salt and pepper. Let it gently cook until you need to serve (I usually cover the pot at this point so that the stock doesn't boil away).

You can also make the soup a day in advance to let the flavours integrate and settle.

# PUMPKIN RAISIN BREAD

## Ingredients

- 2 cups (400 g) sugar
- ⅔ cup (160 ml) oil (sunflower or vegetable)
- 3 eggs
- 1 can pumpkin puree (see note on Frosty Pumpkin Pie)
- ½ cup (120 ml) water
- 2 teaspoons baking soda (bicarbonate of soda)
- 1 teaspoon salt
- 1 teaspoon cinnamon
- 1 teaspoon cloves
- ½ teaspoon US baking powder (see note in the introduction to this chapter)
- 3⅓ cups (430 g) all-purpose (plain) flour
- ½ cup (75 g) raisins or sultanas, plumped up with boiling water

## Directions

1. Grease and flour the bottom and sides of two 9 x 5 x 3 in (33 x 23 x 8 cm) pans (baking tins) or use baking paper to line. Preheat oven to 350°F/180°C/gas mark 4.

2. Mix together sugar, oil, eggs, pumpkin, and water.

3. Mix the dry ingredients in another bowl and add this to the pumpkin mixture. Add the raisins and stir to blend.

4. Pour into prepared pans/baking tins and bake for an hour, or until a skewer inserted near the centre comes out clean. Cool in the pan on a wire rack for 10 minutes, then remove from pan and cool further on the wire rack. Freezes well.

*Makes 2 loaves (serves 32).*

# GREEN SALAD WITH RASPBERRY VINAIGRETTE

## Ingredients

- ½ cup (35 g) sliced almonds
- ¼ cup (50 g) sugar
- ½ head green leaf lettuce
- ½ cup (115 g) diced celery
- 1 cup (175 g) green seedless grapes, halved
- 2 green (spring) onions, chopped
- 1 can (298 g) mandarin oranges, drained
- ½ a cucumber, chopped

## Raspberry Vinaigrette:

- ½ cup (170 g) seedless raspberry jam
- 1 tablespoon runny honey
- ¼ cup (60 ml) red wine or raspberry vinegar
- ⅛ cup (30 ml) fresh lemon juice
- ⅓ cup (80 ml) olive oil
- ¼ teaspoon salt

## Directions

1. Mix the ingredients for the vinaigrette in a blender. Keeps in the fridge for a month, or you can freeze.

2. Cook almonds and sugar over medium heat until sugar caramelizes – stir continually, as the sugar can burn quickly. Transfer to wax paper and cool. Crumble and set aside, trying not to nibble too much.

3. Mix the salad ingredients in a bowl. Toss with dressing prior to serving if you wish, or (my preference) serve the salad and dressing separately. (Americans and Britons tend to like far different amounts of dressing – you can guess who likes more. I always think my British guests will eat more salad than they do; leftover salad keeps much better without dressing on it.)

*Serves 8.*

# BLUEBERRY ORANGE BREAD

## *Ingredients*

- 1 cup (140 g) fresh or frozen blueberries
- 1 tablespoon all-purpose (plain) flour
- 1 teaspoon shredded zest of an orange
- 3 cups (390 g) all-purpose (plain) flour
- 1 cup (200 g) sugar
- 1 tablespoon US baking powder (see note in the introduction to this chapter)
- ½ teaspoon baking soda (bicarbonate of soda)
- ½ teaspoon salt
- 1 egg, beaten
- 1⅓ cup (320 ml) milk
- ¼ cup (60 ml) orange juice*
- ¼ cup (60 ml) oil (sunflower or vegetable)
- 1 teaspoon vanilla extract

*\* If you're making the green salad with the raspberry vinaigrette, you'll have just enough orange juice from the canned mandarin oranges available.*

## *Directions*

1. Grease and flour the bottom and sides of a 9 x 5 x 3 in (23 x 13 x 8 cm) pan (baking tin) or use baking paper to line. Preheat oven to 350°F/180°C/ gas mark 4.

2. Combine blueberries, the tablespoon of flour, and the orange peel in a small bowl, tossing to mix and coat. Set aside.

3. Combine flour, sugar, baking powder, baking soda, and salt. Make a well in the centre and set aside.

4. In another bowl, combine the rest of the ingredients. Add this egg mixture to the well in the dry mixture and stir until the batter is just moistened – the batter will be lumpy. Fold in the blueberry mixture.

5. Place batter into the pan (baking tin) and bake for 45 to 50 minutes, or until a skewer inserted near the centre comes out clean. Cool in the pan on a wire rack for 10 minutes, then remove from pan and cool further on the wire rack.

   *Lovely served with orange cream (soft) cheese – just add some orange juice to cream cheese.*

   *Makes 1 loaf (serves 16).*

# COOKIES

As I say in the Advent/Christmas chapters, Christmas cookies are central to my Christmas celebrations. Here are some of our favourite recipes, but each year I vary which recipes I make, experimenting with new ones. I wish I could avoid making the recipe with cookie cutters (here listed as gingerbread people, but you can use an almond or sugar cookie batter if you wish) because they are so labour intensive, but the kids insist that Christmas wouldn't be the same without them. Many years I'll add white/dark chocolate-covered pretzels, or if I find some peppermint candy canes (which sometimes I've seen at pound shops), I'll crush them into melted white chocolate.

When it comes to cookies, I don't like what we call "cow platters" – those thin, crunchy cookies – but instead prefer smaller soft, chewy cookies. So when I'm baking, to stop the batter spreading, I experiment with how long to chill it, or how much additional flour to add, or with slightly under-baking the dough.

Cookies taste best when they are straight out of the oven, warm and melty. Most can be frozen, but not the chocolate truffles.

An adapted recipe from my grandmother, Nellie Wiese Mohni, whose parents moved from Germany to Iowa in the late 1800s. It is the Pye family favourite:

# ALMOND BURSTS

## Ingredients

- 1 cup (250 g) butter
- 2 teaspoons vanilla extract
- 2 teaspoons almond essence
- ¾ cup (150 g) sugar
- 1 egg
- 3 cups (390 g) all-purpose (plain) flour
- 1 teaspoon nutmeg
- ¼ teaspoon salt

## Frosting (icing):

- ⅓ cup (75 g) butter
- 1 teaspoon vanilla extract
- 2 teaspoons almond essence
- 2 cups (250 g) powdered (icing) sugar
- 2 tablespoons milk

## Directions

1. Cream the first three ingredients; add sugar and blend in the egg.

2. Stir in the rest of the ingredients.

3. Roll the dough into ½ in (1.25 cm) logs about 3 in (7.5 cm) long (or form them into small balls, which is our favourite way).

4. Bake at 350°F/180°C/gas mark 4 for 8–10 minutes on a greased cookie sheet (baking tray).

5. Combine the frosting ingredients and when the cookies are cool, frost (ice) and sprinkle with nutmeg. Try to share with your loved ones.

   *Makes about 36.*

# PEANUT (OR ALMOND) BLOSSOMS

## Ingredients

- ½ cup (125 g) shortening (lard) – or you can use butter
- ½ cup (125 g) peanut (or almond) butter
- 1 egg
- 2 tablespoons milk
- 1 teaspoon vanilla extract
- ½ cup (100 g) sugar
- ½ cup (100 g) light brown sugar
- 1¾ cup (230 g) all-purpose (plain) flour
- ½ teaspoon salt
- 1 teaspoon baking soda (bicarbonate of soda)
- 1 packet chocolate stars or milk buttons or Hershey's kisses (need 48 pieces)

## Directions

1. Cream together shortening or butter, peanut or almond butter, egg, milk, vanilla and sugars.

2. Sift together flour, salt, and soda and add to the wet mixture. Chill.

3. When chilled, shape into 48 balls and roll in sugar. Place on an ungreased cookie sheet (baking tray) and bake for 8–10 minutes at 375°F/190°C/gas mark 5.

4. Remove from oven and press one chocolate into the top of each while still warm.

*Makes 48 cookies.*

# OATMEAL TOFFEE (OR M&M) COOKIES

## Ingredients

- 1 cup (250 g) butter, softened
- 1 cup packed (200 g) light brown sugar
- 2 eggs
- 2 teaspoons vanilla extract
- 2 cups (260 g) all-purpose (plain) flour
- 1 teaspoon baking soda (bicarbonate of soda)
- 1 teaspoon cinnamon
- ½ teaspoon salt
- 3 cups (270 g) oats (old-fashioned/rolled)
- 1¾ cups (roughly 350 g) toffee bits or M&Ms or raisins or chocolate chips

## Directions

1. Heat oven to 375°F/190°C/gas mark 5. Lightly grease cookie sheet (baking tray) or use a non-stick liner, which is what I swear by.

2. Beat butter, brown sugar, eggs and vanilla until blended.

3. Add flour, baking soda, cinnamon, and salt. Beat.

4. Stir in oats and other ingredients as desired. Drop dough by rounded teaspoons onto cookie sheet (baking tray) and bake for 8 to 10 minutes.

*Makes 48 cookies.*

# LEMON POPPY-SEED COOKIES

## Ingredients

- 1 cup (250 g) butter
- 1 cup (200 g) sugar
- 1 egg
- 1 teaspoon vanilla extract
- 2 teaspoons poppy seeds (I use more)
- 1 teaspoon finely shredded lemon zest
- ¼ teaspoon salt
- 2 cups (260 g) all-purpose (plain) flour

## Directions

1. Beat butter for 30 seconds. Add sugar and beat until combined.

2. Beat in egg and vanilla. Then add in poppy seeds, lemon peel, salt, and flour. Chill for an hour or two.

3. Shape into 1 in (2.5 cm) balls. Cook on ungreased cookie sheet (baking tray) for 8–10 minutes in a 375°F/190°C/gas mark 5 oven.

4. Frost with lemon juice mixed with powdered (icing) sugar for an extra pop of lemon. Yum.

*Makes 48 cookies.*

# GINGERBREAD PEOPLE

## Ingredients

- 2¼ cups (290 g) all-purpose (plain) flour
- 1 teaspoon US baking powder (see note in the introduction to this chapter)
- ½ teaspoon salt
- 2 teaspoons cinnamon
- 2 teaspoons ginger
- ¼ teaspoon cloves
- ¼ teaspoon nutmeg
- ¾ cup (185 g) butter
- ½ cup packed (100 g) light brown sugar
- ½ cup (130 g) molasses (can be found online or in big supermarkets in the American section, or you can substitute black treacle)
- 1 egg

## Directions

1. Combine the flour, baking powder, salt, and spices.

2. In a separate bowl, beat butter and brown sugar until light and fluffy. Beat in molasses and egg.

3. Gradually add flour mixture. Beat until well blended. Shape dough into three discs, wrap well and refrigerate for an hour.

4. Preheat oven to 350°F/180°C/ gas mark 4. Working with one disc at a time, roll out on a floury surface. Cut into gingerbread shapes.

5. Bake 10–12 minutes. Cool on wire rack.

6. Ice with buttercream frosting (see the instructions for the Almond Blossoms and leave out the almond essence) or powdered (icing) sugar frosting. Get creative with your decorations – kids love helping out. Your kitchen will be a mess, but think of the memories you'll make.

# OREO TRUFFLES

## Ingredients

- 36 Oreo cookies
- 8 oz (250 g) cream (soft) cheese, softened
- 16 oz (450 g) semi-sweet baking chocolate, melted

## Directions

1. Crush the Oreo cookies (or Bourbons if you can't find Oreos) – crush finely if you prefer a soft interior, or leave big chunks if you prefer some crunch.

2. Add to the cream (soft) cheese, and mix until blended. If you prefer a smooth, non-crunchy interior to your truffle (which I do), chill for an hour.

3. Roll cookie mixture into 1 in (2.5 cm) balls. Dip in melted chocolate (using two forks) and place on wax paper/baking parchment to cool. Refrigerate until firm; about an hour.

*My notes: The first time I made these, for the ingredients I included four 154 g packets of Oreos, half a packet of Bourbon biscuits I had in the house, and two 250 g tubs of soft cheese – one full fat and one half fat. For the melted chocolate, I used up some leftover plain and milk cake covering. But I thought the nicest of the truffles were those made with the fairly traded dark chocolate that I used when I ran out of the others.*

*Make sure you don't scorch the chocolate when you're melting it – I did, even though I thought I was being careful. (Melt in a bowl over gently boiling water.)*

*Makes 48 truffles.*

# A FESTIVE EASTER BRUNCH

When Joshua was a toddler, and would eat whatever we put in front of him, we invited a family with four primary school-aged children over for Easter brunch. The mother apologized afterwards because her kids wouldn't eat any of my offerings, except for the coffee cake and fruit salad. Now that I have kids that age, I see how these items might not appear desirable to a non-adventurous palate – such as my son's now!

If you don't have time to make the amazing cinnamon rolls, a good substitute is coffee cake. And no, there's no coffee in it – it's just a morning-time cake often enjoyed with coffee.

## EGG-AND-SAUSAGE CASSEROLE/BAKE

*("Casserole" in the States refers widely to baked savoury items and not only to stews.)*

### Ingredients

- 1½ lb (700 g) sausage meat (If you can't find packaged sausage meat, or fancy a more flavourful sausage, simply buy your favourite sausages and remove the skins. I like to use Italian sausages, which have zing and flavour.)
- 9 eggs, lightly beaten
- 1½ teaspoons dry mustard
- 1½ cups (200 g) cheddar cheese, grated
- 3 slices bread, cubed (crusts removed if preferred)
- 3 cups (720 ml) milk

### Directions

1. The night before, break up the sausage meat into chunks, fry and drain. In a 13 x 9 in (33 x 23 cm) Pyrex dish add the sausage to other ingredients and mix gently. Leave to soak overnight.

2. Remove from the fridge 1 hour before cooking to bring to room temperature. Bake at 350°F/180°C/gas mark 4 for 45 minutes. The casserole should have a lovely crispy top.

*Serves 8.*

# MOM'S FAMOUS CINNAMON ROLLS

*Inspired by Betty Crocker (She says her sister Judy's are better – it's all about the kneading)*

## Ingredients

- ½ cup (120 ml) warm water (not too hot)
- 1 package of active yeast
- ½ cup (120 ml) milk
- ½ cup (100 g) sugar
- 1 teaspoon salt
- 2 eggs
- ½ cup (125 g) butter or shortening (lard)
- 4½ to 5 cups (600 g) all-purpose (plain) flour

### Filling:

- 2 tablespoons softened butter
- ½ cup (100 g) sugar
- 2 teaspoons cinnamon

### Frosting (icing):

- 1½ to 2 cups (250 g) powdered (icing) sugar
- 1 tablespoon melted butter
- milk to desired consistency

## Directions

1. To the warm water, add the package of yeast and dissolve. Add a dash of sugar to the yeast mixture to help it rise.

2. Melt the butter or shortening (lard) and add it to the milk to raise the temperature of the milk. Stir into the yeast mixture, and then add the sugar, salt, and eggs.

3. Add about 3½ cups (450 g) of the flour to make a sticky dough and, when possible, mix by hand. Turn out onto a floured surface, incorporating much of the rest of the flour. Knead for about five minutes until the dough is smooth and elastic – don't be afraid to work the dough.

4. Place the dough into a greased bowl, greasing the top of it. Cover with a damp cloth and place in a warm area until the dough doubles in size – about an hour and a half. (In our cold vicarage, I turn on the oven for a few minutes on low, turn it off, and put the bowl in there.)

5. Punch the dough down and let rise again until almost double – about 30 minutes.

6. Roll the dough into a rectangular shape, roughly 15 x 9 in (38 x 23 cm). Spread with the softened butter and sprinkle with the sugar and cinnamon. Roll up the dough tightly to form a 15 in (38 cm) roll. Pinch together the edges of the roll to seal, and stretch to even it out where necessary. Cut the roll into 1 in (2.5 cm) slices and place each disc flat side down on a greased 13 x 9 in (33 x 23 cm) pan (baking tin). Make sure you leave some space between each one.

7. Cover and let rise until the dough doubles – about 35 to 45 minutes. Bake for 25 to 30 minutes at 375°F/190°C/gas mark 5.

8. For the frosting (icing), stir together the powdered (icing) sugar and butter, adding enough milk for the desired consistency. If it's too runny, add more powdered sugar; if too thick, add more milk. If it's too runny it will spill off of the rolls, but if it's too thick, it won't spread.

9. Frost (ice) the rolls in the pan while they are still a little warm, spreading across the whole pan.

*These delectable cinnamon rolls are best enjoyed warm, when they melt in your mouth. The Boucher family fights over the middle rolls, all gooey and delicious.*

*Makes 20 cinnamon rolls.*

# CINNAMON COFFEE CAKE

## Ingredients

- ⅔ cup (170 g) butter or shortening (lard)
- 1½ cups packed (300 g) light or dark brown sugar
- 2 eggs, beaten
- 2 cups (260 g) all-purpose (plain) flour
- 1 teaspoon US baking powder (see note in the introduction to this chapter)
- 1 teaspoon baking soda (bicarbonate of soda)
- 1 teaspoon salt
- 1 teaspoon cinnamon
- 1 cup (240 ml) buttermilk (You can make buttermilk easily – for 1 cup (240 ml), place 1 tablespoon of vinegar or lemon juice into your measuring container and fill it the rest of the way with milk. Stir and allow to stand for 5 minutes before using.)

## Topping:

- ½ cup packed (100 g) light or dark brown sugar
- ½ cup (35 g) chopped nuts, if desired
- ½ teaspoon cinnamon

## Directions

1. Mix together butter or shortening (lard) and sugar. Add the eggs and mix well.

2. Sift together the dry ingredients and add to creamed mixture alternately with the buttermilk.

3. Pour into greased and lined 13 x 9 in (33 x 23 cm) pan (baking tin), then sprinkle topping over the batter. Cover with foil and refrigerate overnight.

4. Remove foil and bake at 350°F/180°C/gas mark 4 for 35–40 minutes, or when a skewer comes out clean from the centre of the cake.

   *Serves 8.*

# A FOURTH OF JULY OR FATHER'S DAY BARBECUE OR PICNIC

Okay, so I'd be kidding myself to think that the British would celebrate the Fourth of July. You can use these recipes for any summertime barbecue or picnic, when the days are long and the Pimms is for the sipping.

If you slap some burgers and sausages on the grill, please don't let them be raw on the inside and burnt on the outside! A little patience goes a long way. Following are some wonderful accompaniments to whatever you grill, whether halloumi cheese, salmon, or the old standby, hamburgers. Or if you are going on a picnic, you might want to enjoy my family's famous fried chicken (just please keep it safely chilled). If your only encounter with baked beans has been with the Heinz variety, don't miss out on a truly tasty alternative.

### *Iowa Fried Chicken*

Melt-in-the-mouth fried chicken – wow. My mom, who grew up on a farm in Iowa, remembers: "Mom would raise roosters to sell to the townspeople to eat, and people would order 10 or 15 dressed chickens at a time. So on any given morning, Mother would catch 25 roosters, chop their heads off, and hold them by the feet and wings, letting them bleed out. It was down to me and Judy to dress them – we'd dunk them in scalding water, pick off all of the feathers, remove the insides, wash them again and package them up. We each had our own jobs and didn't complain – we knew this money paid for our school clothes. We'd then fry up a couple of chickens for lunch."

# IOWA FRIED CHICKEN

## *Ingredients*

- 1 whole chicken, cut up
- ½ cup (120 ml) vegetable oil
- 1½ cups (200 g) all-purpose (plain) flour
- Salt and pepper
- Dash of paprika

## *Directions*

1. Cut a whole chicken into pieces – if you need instructions on how to do this, you can find many videos online.

2. Place the flour and seasonings in a plastic sealable bag, and mix together. Piece by piece, coat the chicken in the flour mixture, shaking to cover the pieces completely.

3. In the hot oil, fry the chicken in a cast-iron pan (or something ovenproof) and brown on both sides.

4. When all the pieces are browned, bake in the covered pan at 350°F/180°C/gas mark 4 for an hour. If you want the chicken crispy (and who wouldn't?) remove the lid after half an hour.

*Makes 12 pieces.*

# CORN SALSA

## *Ingredients*

- 2 cups (350 g) sweetcorn (frozen or fresh)
- 1 medium red onion, chopped
- 1 lb (450 g) jar of roasted red peppers, drained and chopped
- 2 tablespoons lime juice
- 1 tablespoon olive oil
- 2 tablespoons cilantro (coriander), chopped
- Salt and pepper, to taste

## *Directions*

1. Heat some olive oil in a cast-iron frying pan over high heat. Add corn, onion, and red peppers; sauté for 5 minutes or until slightly blackened.

2. Place in a bowl and add lime juice, oil, salt and pepper, and cilantro (coriander).

*Serves 8.*

# TEXAS-STYLE BAKED BEANS

## *Ingredients*

- 1 lb (450 g) streaky bacon
- 2 large onions, chopped
- 1 clove garlic
- Canned baked beans with pork sausage (US: 3 cans of 16 oz; UK: 3 cans of 450 g)
- ¼ cup (65 g) dark molasses (can be found online or in big supermarkets in the American section, or you can substitute black treacle)
- ⅓ cup packed (75 g) light brown sugar
- 1 cup (250 g) barbecue sauce

## *Directions*

1. Fry the bacon, remove from the pan, get rid of excess fat, and crumble.

2. In the same pan, using some of the fat from the bacon, sauté the onion and garlic until soft.

3. In an oven-ready casserole dish, such as a cast-iron or ceramic one, add the beans, bacon mixture, and other ingredients. Bake uncovered for 30–40 minutes at 350°F/180°C/gas mark 4, until it bubbles.

*Serves 12.*

# CUCUMBER-DILL SALAD

## Ingredients

- 4 large cucumbers, sliced
- 1 red onion, chopped
- 1 tablespoon dill (dried, or more fresh)
- 1 cup (200 g) sugar
- ½ cup (120 ml) white vinegar
- ½ cup (120 ml) water

## Directions

1. In a large serving bowl, combine cucumbers, onions, and dill.

2. In another bowl, stir together sugar, vinegar, and water; add some salt if desired. Stir until the sugar dissolves and pour over the cucumber mixture.

3. Cover and refrigerate for at least 2 hours before serving.

*Serves 8.*

# FRUIT PIZZA

## *Ingredients*

- 1 sheet puff pastry
- 1–2 280 g tubs cream (soft) cheese
- 2 tablespoons runny honey
- Fruit to decorate

## *Directions*

1. Bake the puff pastry according to the directions (I always make the pizza in a rectangular shape).

2. When it cools, stir together the cream cheese and honey, experimenting with how much you prefer of each. You can also add powdered (icing) sugar if you'd like it sweeter, but I never do.

3. Top the puff pastry with the cheese/honey mixture, and add sliced fruits to decorate. You won't be surprised to learn that on the Fourth of July I make an American flag using strawberries and blueberries. Add some kiwis, cherries, raspberries – use your imagination and get creative.

   *Serves 8.*

# FAVOURITE FAMILY RECIPES

*Passing along recipes over the generations is a gift that I hope will keep on giving. Here are some of our family's favourites, which fit with many occasions.*

## Grandma Wiese's Rye Bread

The idea for the Wiese family cookbook was born when a family member asked for the recipe for Grandma Wiese's rye bread. My great-grandma came to Iowa from Germany in the early part of the century, marrying another German and settling on a farm. Her life was filled with the hard work of cooking, cleaning, gardening and washing clothes – and making rye bread every week. It's not strictly rye bread, however, although in the family parlance it's known as that, but usually made with wholewheat (wholemeal) bread. It's simply amazing.

# RYE BREAD

## Ingredients

- 3⅓ cups (800 ml) lukewarm water (between 110–120°F/ 43–49°C)
- 2 tablespoons yeast
- 1½ tablespoons salt
- 3 tablespoons vegetable oil
- ½ cup (100 g) brown sugar
- 3 cups (375 g) wholewheat (wholemeal) flour
- white flour to knead with

## Directions

1. Add the yeast to the warm water and let stand about 10 minutes. Combine remaining ingredients and add enough white flour to make a sticky dough – this might be as much as 2–3 cups (400 g) of flour.

2. Knead the dough on a floured board for 5 minutes.

3. Place the dough in a greased bowl and cover with a wet tea towel; let rise in a warm place for an hour or until double in size. You might want to use the oven for this; if so, preheat it to 115°F/45°C and then turn the oven off before placing the bowl in it.

4. Grease three 9 x 5 x 3 in (23 x 13 x 8 cm) pans (baking tins). Divide the dough into 3 loaves to fit into the pans. Let them rise until doubled in size and then bake at 350°F/180°C/gas mark 4 for 30 minutes.

   *Makes 3 loaves.*

### *Nellie Mohni's Lemon Meringue Pie*

My maternal grandmother was renowned for her pies; here's one of her signature recipes. A ready-made crust can be substituted for making one from scratch.

# LEMON MERINGUE PIE

## Ingredients

### Crust:

- 1 cup (130 g) all-purpose (plain) flour
- ½ cup (125 g) butter

### Filling:

- ⅓ cup (80 ml) lemon juice
- 1½ cups (300 g) sugar
- 4 tablespoons of cornstarch (cornflour)
- dash of salt
- 4 egg yolks
- 2–3 tablespoons (10–15 g) butter
- 2¼ cups (540 ml) of boiling water

### Meringue:

- 4 egg whites
- 6–8 tablespoons sugar

## Directions

1. To make the crust, mix the flour and butter and pat into a 9 in (23 cm) pie pan and bake at 350°F/180°C/gas mark 4 for 10 minutes.

2. For the filling, blend all of the ingredients except the water in a saucepan. After they are blended, add the boiling water and cook for 3–4 minutes until the mixture is thickened, stirring continually to avoid burning.

3. Make the meringue by beating the egg whites in a clean bowl, starting on medium speed until they start to become thicker, and then adding the sugar gradually, tablespoon by tablespoon. The meringue is done when stiff peaks form.

4. Pour the filling into the partially baked crust. Cover with the meringue and bake at 350°F/180°C/gas mark 4 until the meringue is golden brown – about 15 minutes.

*Makes 6–8 pieces.*

### Mom's Applescotch Pie

My mom is famous for her apple pie, but with recipes for American-as-apple-pie available readily, I've instead included a wonderful applescotch pie, full of flavour.

# APPLESCOTCH PIE

## Ingredients

### Filling:

- 5 cups (5 medium size) apples, peeled and sliced
- 1 cup (200 g) brown sugar, lightly packed
- ¼ cup (60 ml) water
- 1 tablespoon lemon juice
- 2 heaping tablespoons tapioca (a wholegrain that can be ordered online)
- 2 tablespoons sugar
- 1 tablespoon vanilla
- ¾ teaspoon salt
- 3 tablespoons (15 g) butter

### Topping:

- ½ cup (125 g) butter
- ½ cup (100 g) brown sugar, lightly packed
- 1 cup (130 g) all-purpose (plain) flour
- 1 cup (80 g) walnuts, chopped

## Directions

1. In a saucepan, combine apples, brown sugar, water and lemon juice. Cover, cooking slowly for about 7–8 minutes until the apples are just tender.

2. Mix together the tapioca and sugar and add to the apple mixture, stirring constantly until the syrup thickens, about 2 minutes. Remove from the heat, add vanilla, salt and butter, and cool to room temperature.

3. Mix the ingredients for the topping and crumble over the top of the pie. Bake at 400°F/200°C/gas mark 6 for 40–45 minutes.

   *Makes 6–8 pieces.*

## *Dad's Mammoth Ice Cream Cake*

My dad was raised on a farm in southern Minnesota, and when he was 10 his father died, spiralling the family into poverty. Out of this background he retains a practical approach to life – why eat a processed, expensive version of an ice cream cake from a popular chain when you can make your own version better and more cheaply? This recipe is perfect for family birthday feasts.

# ICE CREAM CAKE

## Ingredients

- 14.3 oz (405 g) package Oreo cookies
- 16 oz (450 g) tub ready-to-spread chocolate frosting (buttercream icing)
- ½ gallon (1800 ml) vanilla ice cream (softened)
- ½ gallon (1800 ml) chocolate ice cream (softened)
- 1 cup (120 ml) milk approximately

## Directions

1. Before you start, make sure you can assemble all of the ingredients quickly because the ice cream soon makes a melty, sloppy mess.

2. Crush all of the Oreo cookies, except 5, in a bowl. Add the milk gradually and stir to make a slurry – a mixture the consistency of a thick cake batter. Fold in the chocolate frosting (icing). Set aside.

3. Spread the chocolate ice cream evenly into the bottom of a 9-in (23 cm) springform pan. Spoon in the Oreo slurry. On top, add the softened vanilla ice cream. You'll discover that the pan will not hold the full amount of the vanilla ice cream, so you will need to pile it up toward the middle.

4. Crush the remaining Oreo cookies and sprinkle them on the top. Cover with aluminium foil and freeze for several hours or overnight.

   *Makes 32 standard servings – but most people eat 3–4 servings per slice!*

# ACKNOWLEDGEMENTS

I burst with gratitude when I think of the many people cheering me along as I wrote this book in my long and winding road to publication.

For Nicholas, my biggest fan, who never fails to encourage me on in my writing, and in life. For our kids, whom we love so much and are so proud of. We're cheering you on as you launch into your adult lives.

For Steve Mitchell, my original publishing champion and mentor, who helped me release this book and who still encourages me regularly. I'm so grateful.

For the writing friends who have kept me going: Michele Guinness, who all those years ago simply said, "Amy, just tell your story." To Tanya Marlow and Amy Scott Robinson, some of my besties who stand with me in all of my writing and in life, helping me to go deeper and to be clearer. For Jennie Pollock, my editor and friend, who compelled me, gracefully, to dig deeper, to push harder, and to kill those darlings whose screams would reverberate only in my heart.

For Julie and Mike Jowett, who provided a welcoming place to write in the sunshine at El Palmeral in Spain, with sumptuous food and even better conversation.

For my reader reviewers, who cheered me on and boosted my confidence as I wrote my first book: Leo and Phyllis

Boucher, Sue Brouwer, Pam Burke, Esther Clift, Julia Evans, Shona Minson, Candy O'Donovan, Sharon Roberts, Alie Teale, Margaret Vaughan, Chris Vickery, and Julia Wilson.

For my church community, who keep me rooted and accountable, and my prayer-warrior friends, Ali Grafham and Anne LeTissier, to whom and through whom God speaks.

For Vivian Hansen, who designed the iconic first cover and now has knocked it out of the park with this one too. I love that our book publishing journeys have so many parallels. Thank you for exercising your gifts and creativity in bringing books to life.

For the amazing Authentic team. Thank you for taking a chance on me a decade ago and now for releasing this special anniversary edition; I'm exceedingly grateful. Thank you to Donna Harris with her leadership, Rachael Franklin for all things sales and marketing, Claire Gough for wrangling the old and new together editorially, and for all of the members of the team. What a joy to work with you!

# NOTES

## Introduction: A Stranger in a Foreign Land

[1]  I did so with the help of the ministry of Leanne Payne and her books such as *Restoring the Christian Soul* (Grand Rapids: Baker, 1996).

[2]  Psalm 119:103.

[3]  US: church minister.

[4]  US: British roads are classified, from the biggest to the smallest, as motorways (like the interstate), dual carriageways (divided highways, but with slightly different rules to a motorway), A roads (often divided highways with two lanes in each direction – but not always), B roads (single-lane roads), and then the network of streets, lanes, and alleyways. A winding explanation? Rapeseed is similar to canola. A cream tea is afternoon tea with scones, clotted cream, and jam. National Trust house: a stately home (think Downton Abbey), bequeathed to a charity called the National Trust when the family could no longer afford the upkeep or the taxes. They are open to the public and make popular destinations for days out. (See the chapter on "The Rhythm of Rest" for more.) Chips are chunky, greasy fries – a far cry from those served by fast-food chains.

## 1  "More Tea, Vicar?"

[1]  Okay, really? Britons call a sweater vest a tank top? I had no idea. A tank top to Americans is a sleeveless T-shirt worn in summertime.

[2]  With thanks to Ellen Flack, Jacqueline Pye, Sharon Roberts, and Lucy Mills.

3  With thanks to Maureen Chapman.
4  See Matthew 10:42.
5  Roy Goodwin and Dave Roberts, *The Grace Outpouring* (Colorado Springs, CO: David C Cook, 2008).
6  US: not those things served with gravy in the South, but cookies – yet biscuits here are usually crisp and crunchy, not soft and chewy.

## 2  The Day They Buried Diana

1  The District of Columbia – DC, as it's shortened.
2  UK: boot. As we'll explore in the chapter on accents and language, cars have so many different words associated with them – windshield/windscreen, hood/bonnet, side mirror/wing mirror . . .
3  US: seminary.
4  US: a curate is a Church of England minister who most often serves an apprenticeship period of three to four years.
5  UK: housemate.

## 3  School Days

1  US: vacations.
2  Au pairs – a delightful European convention where a young adult, often from abroad, is hosted by a family as a cultural exchange. The au pair helps with childcare and light cleaning while getting the chance to practise language skills and experience a new culture. Our big vicarage enabled us to embrace this so we could have the kids at home but I could do my publishing work too. My house was never so clean as with our gorgeous German au pairs.
3  US: roughly the same as first grade, although kids start in school at four years old with what's called reception, then year one, and so on.
4  US: elementary school.
5  US: secondary school starts at about the same age as middle school or junior high, but students can stay until they are 18, depending on whether their school provides GCSEs and A-levels. Huh? I know – I won't even begin to define those.
6  US: sidewalk.
7  US: trucks.

8   US: the UK governing body that sets the standards for schools and then sees how individual schools are faring. The specific timing of inspections isn't told to a school in advance, so an impending inspection can produce a massive amount of stress. Teachers have one chance – one lesson – to prove they are doing a good job, with, for instance, an immaculate class-room, informative and creative displays, and up-to-date written records on the children's progress.

## 4   "We Will Remember"

1   Nicholas found the story while researching online. For instance, see http://www.ww1battlefields.co.uk/somme/ulstertower.html (accessed 22/04/2025).

## 5   Bringing in the Sheaves

1   *The Book of Common Prayer* (New York: Church Publishing, 1979), 194.
2   US: acquisitions.
3   US: A "hackney carriage" is the official name of the iconic black London taxi.
4   UK: Many Americans serve a sweet-potato dish topped with marshmal-lows on Thanksgiving. I believe the (questionable!) practice evolved as the dish morphed from a sweet-potato pie into a side dish served with the turkey. At the turn of the twentieth century, marshmallows were considered modern and labour-saving.
5   As found on the blog of Robert Tracy McKenzie, professor and chair of the Department of History at Wheaton College, https://faithandamericanhistory.wordpress.com/2014/11/20/when-fiction-becomes-fact-the-novel-that-taught-americans-about-the-first-thanksgiving/ (accessed 22/04/2025).
6   Ambassador Matthew Barzun's remarks at the Thanksgiving service at St Paul's Cathedral, 27 November 2014.
7   US: Marmite, that love-it-or-hate-it nasty brown and sticky spread, made of yeast extract.

8   Recipes for a Thanksgiving feast – and the other wonderful foods I mention in chapters below – can be found at the end of the book. I'd love to hear if you make them – please post on my website (www.amyboucherpye.com) or social media feed.

9   US: defying belief.

10  See http://blackfridaydeathcount.com.

11  US: Primark is a large discount department store that sells its own brands, and has been criticized for the factory conditions in foreign countries making its clothes, following the collapse of the Rana Plaza factory in Bangladesh in 2013. Soon Primark, an Irish company, will open in the States.

12  US: canned.

13  With thanks to Steve Clough.

14  Check out her wonderful books, such as *It's Just You and Me, Lord*.

15  After Hosea 10:12.

16  I'm sorry I can't give you the source for this prayer; it's one Nicholas found among his many resources. We thought it might appear in the US 1979 version of *The Book of Common Prayer*, but evidently not. It's very close to the "Grace at Meals" found there: "Give us grateful hearts, our Father, for all thy mercies, and make us mindful of the needs of others; through Jesus Christ our Lord. Amen."

## 6   Life as a VW

1   US: the Home Counties are those which surround London, often prosperous, and inhabited by many commuters to London.

2   US: rest area or travel plaza. Yep, overpriced here just as there.

3   Available in the UK from Costco. My secret's out.

4   Because I had been married previously to an ordinand, then a curate. Same guy.

5   US: nursery.

6   US: driveway. These minute changes in language I found disconcerting at first.

7   With thanks to the apostle Paul for his poetic language.

## 7   Waiting for the Coming King

[1] Shepherds or sailors, a saying that goes back to Shakespeare and even Jesus in Matthew 16:2–3, when he notes that the religious leaders can interpret the appearance of the sky in terms of the weather.

## 8   The Light of Christ Has Come into Our World

[1] US: attic.
[2] My mom. Legend.
[3] US: appetizer.
[4] US: garbage truck. The British also call this a dustcart, which mystifies me.
[5] With thanks to Geraldine Buckley, master storyteller. Boxing Day, for those unfamiliar, is 26 December, a public holiday in Britain. Traditionally it was when servants would receive a Christmas box from those upstairs.

## 9   The New Year Dawns

[1] US: trash cans and trash.
[2] With thanks to Dorothy Courtis and Lucy Lewis.
[3] See my blog for an article I wrote for *Woman Alive* on how to keep a spiritual journal: http://www.amyboucherpye.com/2015/01/07/how-to-keep-a-spiritual-journal-a-treasure-trove-of-gods-love/ (accessed 22/04/2025).
[4] US: not a journal, but a calendar.
[5] *My One Word: Change Your Life with Just One Word.* Mike Ashcraft and Rachel Olsen (Grand Rapids, MI: Zondervan, 2012). Also see www.myoneword.org.
[6] Check out her website, *Thorns and Gold*, for some thought-provoking articles: www.tanyamarlow.com.

## 10   Come to My Party!

[1] UK: a lay leader of the church.
[2] Can you tell how much I prize her? I got to know her when editing her magnum opus *Woman: The Full Story*, which was released as

*The Contemporary Woman: Can she really have it all?* (London: Hodder, 2021). I was thrilled to add a preface to the new edition.

3  US: Yes, this needs defining. The children sit in a circle and pass around a gift wrapped in many layers of paper, with a small treat in between each layer. The leader plays music, which stops (supposedly randomly – the leader is not supposed to look, but part of his or her job is to try to make sure every child gets a turn) and the child holding the parcel then unwraps a layer. Having taken their treat, they pass the parcel to the next person when the music starts again. The trick for the leader, of course, is to remember who has received a treat and who hasn't – and to make sure that the big treat at the end isn't won by the birthday person. Usually some level of confusion reigns.

4  Dallas Willard, *The Spirit of the Disciplines* (San Francisco, CA: Harper & Row, 1988), 179. I smiled when I recently saw the front flyleaf, for I got to meet Dallas a few times in my work with the Trinity Forum, and had forgotten that he signed this copy. After his name, he put James 3:17, which is "But the wisdom that comes from heaven is first of all pure; then peace-loving, considerate, submissive, full of mercy and good fruit, impartial and sincere." He's enjoying the ultimate of celebrations and the wisdom of heaven now; what an amazing man.

## 11  By Their Accent Shall Ye Know Them

1  UK: queue. Target doesn't have queues in my parlance.

2  UK: rubbers in the States are condoms.

3  See "Translation table explaining the truth behind British politeness becomes Internet hit," Alice Philipson, *The Telegraph*, 2 September 2013. Available online.

4  US: know this phrase? Knickers equal underwear, so it means getting overly concerned about something often insignificant.

5  US: in your face.

6  Kate Fox, *Watching the English* (London: Hodder & Stoughton, 2004). Her book applies to England, and not necessarily all of Britain.

7  Great word, American friends; it means staying silent. Has roots in the German word stumm but spelled as it is because it is Yiddish, as Michele Guinness told me. She says, "In fact, Americans adopted lots of Yiddish words – many more than the Brits – so you have schmaltz

(chicken fat), schlep, schmuck and schmooze, all largely unknown here." Fascinating – I know all of those words she mentions, but didn't realize they didn't appear on these shores.

8   US: Received Pronunciation (RP), is the upper-class accent – think of those upstairs on *Downton Abbey*. It's also sometimes called "BBC English" for reasons we'll explore later.

9   US: principal.

10  I didn't explore the public school system in the education chapter, but unlike in America, where public schools are funded by taxpayers, public schools over here are private institutions serving an elite clientele. Think Eton, where princes William and Harry attended, for instance.

11  With thanks to Lavonne Neff and Diane Komp, both wise, outward-looking Americans.

12  Yep, Cheryl Cole. She now goes by her maiden name.

13  See Genesis 11:1–9.

## 12   "Behold Your King!"

1   US: rental car. And I certainly didn't drive, Nicholas did. Although I now have a British licence, driving in this country ranks high on my list of least favourite things. At least now we have GPS devices that keep me from being completely lost.

2   Walter Wangerin, *Reliving the Passion* (Grand Rapids, MI: Zondervan, 1992).

3   My second book flowed out of this idea: *The Living Cross: Exploring God's Gift of Forgiveness and New Life* (Abingdon: BRF, 2016).

## 13   Being Easter People

1   Tom Wright, *Surprised by Hope* (London: SPCK, 2007), 268.

2   With thanks to Elaine Kemp.

3   With thanks to Maureen Chapman.

4   With thanks to Julia Wilson. US: A wally is a term for an inept person.

5   The indwelling Christ – a favourite theme of mine. Paul's letters burst with references; see, for instance, Colossians 1:27, 2 Corinthians 5:17, or 2 Corinthians 13:5.

6  Tom Wright, *Surprised by Hope*, 269.
7  *Ibid.*
8  I'm referencing the story according to John 21.
9  Conrad Gempf, *Mealtime Habits of the Messiah* (Grand Rapids, MI: Zondervan, 2005), 18.
10 *Ibid.*, 19.
11 *Ibid.*

## 14  Festival Time

1  I was intrigued to hear the reason why, in 2015, Spring Harvest moved the Minehead meetings into the Skyline space. Not to save money, as many people thought, but because the Environment Agency had received a handful of complaints about noise levels and said they would shut down the gathering if anyone else complained.

2  Attendance has fallen from those years: in the nineties some 70,000 people attended, whereas in 2015 it was 20,000. But organizers say the numbers are no longer dropping. Many events are struggling in the years after the financial meltdown of 2007–8.

3  US: a wonderful word to employ, meaning pleased and puffed up in a good way.

4  When this book was first published, it was known as the Man Booker Prize, but now is the International Booker Prize.

5  US: gentle slang for customers or clients.

6  US: Skegness is one of the locations for Spring Harvest.

7  US: Wellington boots, or gumboots.

## 15  Plumbing the Depths

1  UK: yes, the ladies'. This was way before I would try to figure out what to call the loo.

2  Helene Hanff, *84 Charing Cross Road* (Aylesbury: Futura, 1976), 109. This excerpt is from *The Duchess of Bloomsbury Street*, which is included in this edition of *84 Charing Cross Road*.

3  You can find these interesting bits of history from a plumbing firm: https://www.victorianplumbing.co.uk/bathroom-ideas-and-inspiration/why-do-we-say-going-to-the-loo (accessed 25/04/2025).

4  US: a single-pane window.

5  US: secondary glazing is an extra layer of window (glass) installed inside the house and separate from the outer window.

6  US: attic.

7  US: faucets.

## 16   Rain, Rain, Go Away . . .

1  You were thinking of this quotation, weren't you: "When a man is tired of London, he is tired of life."

2  Kate Fox, *Watching the English* (London: Hodder & Stoughton, 2004), 33.

3  *Ibid.*

4  US: I can't translate "high street" easily. The American "main street" in old-fashioned towns would equate, but in the land of the sprawling suburbia one can't just dash out on foot for milk and bread anyway.

5  US: backyard.

6  US: an English fruity spirit-based drink.

7  Found online at https://thecatholicherald.com/the-sun-newspaper-asks-readers-to-pray-to-french-bishop-to-stop-the-rain/ (accessed 25/04/2025).

8  Agnes Sanford, *Creation Waits* (Plainfield, NJ: Logos International, n.d.), 1–3. As quoted in Leanne Payne, *Heaven's Calling* (Grand Rapids, MI: Baker, 2008), 254.

9  *Ibid.*

10  These stories are all in *Heaven's Calling*, pages 252–57, which I recommend.

11  US: to talk, wheedle, or cajole your way into something.

## 17   The Rhythm of Rest

1  The European approach to holidays is one I've gladly adopted. So many American companies have a stingy holiday/vacation policy, sometimes

only allowing two weeks off – a far cry from the UK government-imposed minimum of twenty days of paid holiday, plus Bank Holidays, for full-time workers.

2   US: The British even call the backyard a garden.

3   Kate Fox, *Watching the English* (London: Hodder & Stoughton, 2004), 131.

4   UK: tenpin. Americans generally don't speak of other types of bowling.

5   Karl Dahlfred, 25 November 2014, "Why Missionaries Can Never Go Home Again" on the "Gleanings from the Field" blog, http://www.dahlfred.com/index.php/blogs/gleanings-from-the-field/747-why-missionaries-can-never-go-home-again (accessed 22/04/2025).

## 18   What's in a Name?

1   Kate Fox, *Watching the English* (London: Hodder & Stoughton, 2004), 39.

2   With thanks to those who took part in the conversation on Facebook and my blog, http://www.amyboucherpye.com/2014/04/04/life-in-the-uk-the-no-name-rule/#comments: Jennie Pollock, Bev Murrill, Ase Johannessen, Hannah Brown, Catherine Davies van Zoen, Maureen Chapman, and Amber Salladin.

3   US: figured out.

4   See Psalm 62:1–2.

5   I've been helped in uncovering this imagery especially by Craig Keener in the *NIV Application Commentary* (Grand Rapids: Zondervan, 2000), 126–27.

6   After Isaiah 62:2–5.

## 19   Queuing, and Other British Sports

1   With thanks to my friend, who wishes to remain unnamed. Swim club politics and all of that.

2   US: commercials.

3   Known as the home of cricket. The first match was played at Lord's in 1787.

4   MV Hughes, *About England* (London: JM Dent & Sons, 1927), 338.

5   As earlier, it's soccer.
6   See the interesting article by Dave Roberts, "Aston Villa and the Mission of God," *Christianity*, June 2010, 32, 35–38.
7   MV Hughes, *About England*, 332.
8   Amanda van Mulligan, "The British Art of Queuing": https://turn-ingdutch.com/2014/04/04/the-british-art-of-queuing-on-smitten-by-britain/ (accessed 25/04/2025).

## 20   Parallel Lives

1   Her books are well worth reading: *High Heels and Holiness*, *Real Life, Real God*, and *Influential* – all published by Hodder in the UK (IVP in the States).
2   US: sidewalks.

## Epilogue: Liquid Love

1   See Luke 10:38 and following.
2   After Isaiah 55.

## Afterword: Looking Back and Ahead with Gratitude and Hope

1   US: elementary school. I also write about hearing God with this story in "Hearing God," *7 Ways to Pray* (London: SPCK and Colorado Springs: NavPress, 2021), 65. For a full list of my books, visit my website: amy-boucherpye.com.
2   US: a distinction is the highest grade awarded; below that is merit and then pass.
3   "Patient Trust," Pierre Teilhard de Chardin, SJ, excerpted in Michael Harter, *Hearts on Fire: Praying with Jesuits* (Chicago: Loyola Press, 2005). See https://www.ignatianspirituality.com/prayer-of-theilhard-de-chardin/ (accessed 22/04/2025).

4   I write about this in *Transforming Love: How Friendship with Jesus Changes Us* (London: SPCK and Grand Rapids: Our Daily Bread Publishing, 2023), 65–66.

5   See Deuteronomy 33:27.

6   I love this way of praying so much that I included it at the end of each chapter of *Transforming Love*. For more prayer practices, join my YouTube channel (just search my name) and my monthly newsletter list: https://tinyurl.com/amyprayernewsletter.

7   The Church of England splits itself up into geographical parishes, with (in the past) one church per parish. My husband as a historian and lover of all things Anglican, already could tell you the boundaries of his new parish. Not that many of those within it would be aware of this classification!

8   Hebrews 3:4.

9   CS Lewis, *Mere Christianity* (New York: Macmillan, 1943), 174.

# JOIN THE CONVERSATION!

I love getting to know readers online and in person, and I love hearing your stories – especially of how you find home. Here's where you can find me:

Join my monthly newsletter: https://tinyurl.com/amyprayernewsletter

Website: amyboucherpye.com

Email: amy@amyboucherpye.com

Facebook: Amy Boucher Pye

Instagram: amyboucherpye

YouTube (for prayer practices): Amy Boucher Pye

www.ingramcontent.com/pod-product-compliance
Ingram Content Group UK Ltd.
Pitfield, Milton Keynes, MK11 3LW, UK
UKHW021419041025
463586UK00005B/9

9 781788 934459